JUMP START

How to Get Your Life Together **NOW**
Working on your dreams for the **FUTURE**

BETA READING COPY ONLY
Second manuscript
PROOFREADING AND CONTENT EDITING IS
INCOMPLETE

Thank you Renee! I love your enthusiasm and good vibes!

12/03/2021

FERNANDO EID PIRES

Fernando Eid Pires

Jumpstart
Copyright © 2021 by Fernando Eid Pires

All rights reserved. No part of this book may be reproduced or transmitted in any form or by any means, graphic, electronic, or mechanical, including photocopying, recording, taping, or by any information storage or retrieval system, without the written permission of the copyright owner. For permissions, please write to: fpiresllc@gmail.com

ISBN: 978-1-7377393-0-2

Printed in the United States of America, 2021.
Beta reading, 2nd manuscript – not published.

CONTENTS

Background:

Where the heck do I come from!? 5

Acknowledgements 17

There's no distance between you and me. 20

Chapters:

1. What is YOUR definition of success? 22

2. Your Valuable Time 26

3. Your Body Temple 31

4. Physical Energy 37

5. Your Emotional Bank Account 43

6. Self Esteem 50

7. Beliefs 57

8. Setting Worthwhile Goals 62

   Bonus: From Student Loan to Financial Freedom 67

9. Your Habits 76

10. Taking ACTION 81

11. Leveraging Failure 86

12. Dealing with Criticism 91

13. Work Ethic 96

14. Leadership at the Workplace 100

15. Using Gratification well 105

16. How to become UNSTOPPABLE 110

17. Unlocking the Power of Your Mind 118

18. SIDE HUSTLE! 124
19. The "Nine to Five" Job 129
20. Getting a RAISE 135
21. Money Management 140
22. Imagination & Creativity 146
23. Create Value 151
24. Fundamentals of Products and Services 156
25. DISRUPT your approach! 163
26. Finding your ROMANTIC partner! 168
27. The Plan TODAY 180

The Pitfalls of Society:

1. Societal Auto-immune Disease 189
2. Pornography and Human Trafficking 193
3. Unhealthy Financial System 200

Motivational Quotes and Nuggets of Wisdom:

By the Author 213
By other Authors and Leaders 214

JUMPSTART

Background

12 pages | 20 minutes

Where the heck do I come from!?

I prematurely came into this world in the city of São Paulo, Brazil. Right off the bat I struggled for my life in the ICU with incomplete formed lungs, and consequently, pneumonia. My parents fought like Tom & Jerry, and when I was only two years old, they divorced.

My mother had custody of me and she was doing her best, but she was an emotional wreck. Money was extremely short, and we've experienced scarcity to the point that my mom sometimes could only make one plate for the both of us. She would let me eat first, and whatever I left there, she would finish. I never went hungry, but both my parents did occasionally. They would fight like junkyard dogs over who should pay for this or that, so money was the big elephant in the room from day one. In fact, not only I never got a chance to see my parents happily married, but I actually saw my entire family crumble over money matters. At the age of seven I stood naked in front of a full-size mirror, taking a good, hard look at myself head to toes, and promised that I would do the whole thing differently, VERY differently and much better.

While my father was a *rolling stone*, my mother was extremely uptight and rigid. Because she was afraid that I could turn out to be like my father, she did not hesitate to severely punish me for the smallest of things that I would do "wrong"—it was a military regime at home. With my father, it was the extreme opposite; I could do anything I wanted, go out and fly a kite, play soccer out on the streets, etc. At the same time that I loved the freedom, I hated the complete lack of structure he had.

It was a mindfuck, as there was no such thing as balance—it was one extreme or the other extreme. As I lived mostly with my mother, and because I was too overwhelmed by the rules of the house, I sheltered myself in my little bubble learning electronics by trial and error—because the internet wasn't a thing yet. I was only four years old when I became obsessed with it. I wanted to spend my time literally just minding my business, because home wasn't a very happy place. I remember trying so hard to figure out how those electronic components worked, that I literally had sweat drip from my head even though the room temperature was cool. That's how much I was forcing my brain to think. I had severe migraines at least a few times a week, it was a normal thing to me.

At school I was seen and treated as an abomination. At the age of seven or eight I didn't play much, I talked pretty much like an adult, I reasoned like an adult, and felt like one. The kids bullied me, in fact, most of my school time I was severely bullied. This only changed when I began to be more assertive and create hard boundaries, which took me a while, since I was always the smallest kid in the classroom. The teachers also bullied me, one of them in pre-school even motivated the class to keep away from me and make me completely isolated. My level of anxiety was such that I felt like an elephant was sitting on my chest all day long, it literally did hurt so painfully that it was hard to breathe at times. I lived in a state of alertness as if someone was coming at me with a knife—I had no rest. The only time I felt better was when I was locked in my room, playing with my electronics stuff. At the age of 12 I came extremely close to running away from home, I just never had the balls to do it.

Not all was bad, though. At the age of 15, I was making my own money by building and selling computers, as well as I had a pretty cool peer of friends. We would laugh every day so hard that our guts would hurt and it would be difficult to catch a breath! That was the year of 2003, pretty much the year that I laughed the most ever, and perhaps the happiest time of my life to this day. At the age of 18, I went to college for 3 months and ditched it. With $5,000.00 Reais (Brazilian currency) that I borrowed from my grandpa Toufic (te amo jida), I started my company Acousticlass Audio at the end of 2005. My grandpa believed in me, he often said "this boy is going places."

My grandpa helping me set up my first "office" in the back of a house. Te amo vovô.

I had the time of my life working myself to exhaustion but doing what I absolutely love to death. At the same time, my high school friends and I were tearing up the city at night. Fun times!

That utopia lasted until the age of 21, when I came close to having a heart attack for being extremely stressed and frustrated with how things work in Brazil. It was 2009 when I actually saw the customs working at the port, where I personally went to pick up the electronic components that I had imported myself from China. I was disgusted by what I saw. That year, the president of Brazil was Lula, perhaps the most corrupt human to ever fart on a presidential chair. Right there and then, I decided to leave Brazil and never, ever look back. It took me seven years, but I've done it the right way.

Between the years of 2009 and 2012, I manufactured, sold, shipped and supported the warranty of my products, more in particular, the LiveClass portable P.A. system.

Introducing the LiveClass to the open public in the Expo Music 2008.

It was a grind. At the same time I was doing that, I was also studying and trying really hard to get a scholarship at the University of Miami, as they have Music and Audio Engineering programs that really interested me. That did not work out, as no matter how extraordinary my real-world achievements were, the admission committee simply would not allow me to study at their campus because of my crappy high school grades—even if I paid the full tuition that I could not afford.

At the same time, I visited Peavey Electronics twice with different prototypes, the first time in 2010, and the second time in 2011. The first time I visited them, along with the "LiveClass," I also brought the "StudioAmp"—an invention that was freaking huge. I dragged all of its 130 lbs from Brazil all the way to Meridian in Mississippi. Once we met, it took about five minutes for me to find out that I was way off with my invention, and it had no real-world value. Then I spent the remaining nine days there feeling guilty and grieving about how terribly wrong things were going.

JUMPSTART

The "StudioAmp" prototype weighing over 130 lbs all packed up.

However, I did see how they design their products and became determined to do a phenomenal job at creating something that, perhaps even they couldn't. And I did exactly that.

The second time I visited Peavey in 2011, I brought the StudioMotion to them, which was an absurd evolution over the previous LiveClass system they first saw. This time, the housing of it wasn't made of wood, but of plexiglass instead.

The StudioMotion—to this day, one of the best portable P.A. systems in the world.

It looks pretty amazing, but the real reason behind the plexiglass idea, was that I feared that the second time around knocking on their door, they wouldn't take me seriously and wouldn't give me the chance to show the amazing engineering inside of this new piece of equipment. I figured that if it was transparent, then they would see inside of it right away and be really impressed. Well, that worked like a charm. As soon as they laid eyes on it, their jaw dropped and they took me in immediately. My intent was to sell them the design, get a nice big check for it, then go study at the University of Miami. They didn't want to buy the design because it wasn't an invention protected by a patent, however, they did offer me an excellent job at their beautiful headquarters. I wasn't ready to move to a tiny town in Mississippi and felt that I had a lot more to learn before getting a job and settling down, so I passed on it.

In 2012 I flew to Miami in hopes to meet the folks that could recognize my extraordinary abilities and get a scholarship to learn something called DSP (digital signal processing). That did not work at all. One month roaming around the campus, showing them my products and shaking hands, resulted in nothing. With my tail between my legs, I went back to Brazil for the third time empty handed. Actually, not empty handed, I went back there with a bunch of DSP books. I almost desperately wanted to be there to learn such thing, but I figured... As with everything else, I would freaking teach it to myself again.

By the end of 2013, I had already developed a new product, the CarDSP, purely based on this revolutionary DSP technology. It was this rather discrete looking black box that, by connecting to your computer, allowed you to tune the sound system of your car to the finest degree. Yes, that's right. I wanted to spend about five years at the University of Miami only to learn DSP, but in less than two years by myself alone I've learned it AND developed a sophisticated DSP product. Initially I didn't think I could pull that off, but once again, I was better off learning things on my own. This product was so advanced at the time, that only a handful of companies in the world had something like it, including Alpine. It was highly desirable and of high value. What no one knew is that I developed it out of my tiny bedroom in Brazil, dripping sweat on the keyboard while coding with no air conditioning and drinking ungodly amounts of coffee to "motivate" myself, as I was depressed at that time.

My tiny bedroom. Two office desks, one bed and no space. I spent over two years in that room almost 24/7, creating the CarDSP. It took a toll on my mental health.

The first few CarDSP produced. I also packed, sold and shipped them.

Upon finishing this audacious DSP project, I felt that I had gold in my hands. To hopefully sell this "gold," I spent a week in my grandpa's garage making a video presentation of it, as professionally as possible, with the goal to negotiate it with a reputable company that had the capacity to manufacture and distribute it in exchange for royalties.

The "movie set" I built to shoot the movie of the AudioSigma CarDSP.

What the movie looked like, and the dark circles around my eyes!

As a result, a rather small company from Los Angeles reached out and the owner convinced me to fly to L.A. to negotiate terms and help them get the production going. I thought I had nothing to lose, and I did as he proposed. What this man saw was a very intelligent, somewhat naive, financially stranded young boy that he could take advantage of. The time I spent in L.A. was pretty terrible, poorly lodged in a bedroom in a low-income neighborhood and spending my own money to survive there.

Actually, not my own money, but my mother's; she was transferring money to me "just until the business deal happens"—but the truth is that there was no deal, only lies. This man also tried to convince me to stay in the U.S. past the period that I was legally allowed to remain in the country. I might've been in the worst shape of my life, but I had my dignity, so I packed all my stuff and went back to Brazil. Long story short, they manufactured and sold my product by the hundreds, if not thousands, and never paid me a single dollar for it. So much for not having anything to lose... Joke's on them though, as they had so many quality related production issues that I doubt they made a significant profit on it—Karma is a b*tch.

For the fourth time I arrived back in Brazil, this time not only empty handed like before, but at great loss. I was broke, and literally watching them sell my own product with their brand, while giving me nothing in return. It was infuriating. I only had TWO thousand dollars to my name, and therefore, it was the end of the line—I had to get a job. Age was also starting to weigh on me.

Although I had "failed" so miserably multiple times, I've always done a masterful job creating something desirable and selling it. No one has ever rejected something I created. Customers were always happy to pay for it and spread a good word about the very thing they bought with their hard-earned money—the thing that was a manifestation of my imagination. Both the "creating" and the "selling" parts were never, ever a problem. Problems were logistics, cash flow, manufacturing, supply chain, etc., but I was a damn good creator and seller. The problem was, at that point I had no-*thing* else to sell except... MYSELF!

I went about advertising myself for a job like I would do for any of my products. By the end of 2015, I sent out a video to several companies in the U.S. and Brazil, demonstrating all my "features"—that being everything that I could actually DO for them. Unlike a normal and boring C.V. in which I would just list my experiences, I actually SHOWED myself doing the things I do, using electronic design softwares, soldering tiny electronic components on beautiful circuit boards, coding software, and showing finished products that were the result of all that state-of-the-art work.

RESULT. The first email came within three short hours of sending out the video, and guess what, it was from Kicker—my current employer. They seemed to be very interested. They asked me something like "Okay, you know all these things. But to what degree do you know them? What's your level of expertise on these things?" It just so happens that it was a question I could not answer in full honesty, because I had no idea if what was good for me, was good enough according to their standards. So, I proposed the following: "How about I build you a prototype to the best of my abilities exclusively for you guys, ship it over there, then YOU tell me how good or not good I am at doing this stuff?" Of course, they agreed.

Then, out of the two thousand bucks I had, I spent $1,400.00 to build the prototype, plus another good chunk to ship it. I worked my ASS off designing something from scratch in less than two months, that normally would've taken at least half of a year for Kicker to do the same. Once I was finished building it, I went to the nearest FedEx location, closed my eyes and shipped the damn thing. For over 10 days after the tracking showed "delivered," I still haven't heard anything from them. Despite that, I restrained myself from following up to not seem needy or desperate. Then, after this long and anxious wait, this *one liner* email came: "Do I need a VISA to go interview you in Brazil?"

JUMPSTART

The prototype I built in my bedroom, exclusively for Kicker, as proof of my skills.

I figured, if they're willing to literally go that distance to interview me, then they must've liked what they saw. Long story short, I already had a Visa to enter the U.S., so we talked on a Thursday and they booked me a flight for Sunday of the same week. That was nuts.

There I went, for a job interview overseas, and the 5th entry in the U.S. was stamped on my passport in December of 2015. No, none of those entries were to visit Disneyland. The four-day job interview went great. They did not give me any hopes or made any promises that they couldn't keep—unlike the shady company from L.A.

Mr. Irby and Jay, president and vice-president of Kicker, had taken me out to the nicest burger joint in Stillwater—Eskimo Joe's. They were cheerful and kind and made me very comfortable. The vibe was great, the humor was awesome. The fourth and last day, they took me to the city of Norman to see immigration lawyers and get a realistic opinion of whether there was any way I could become a permanent resident of the U.S., as not having a degree added more strain to the already difficult process. The lawyers came up with a good plan, using my company in Brazil. It worked out great, and in less than two years, I got my Green Card.

Back in Brazil after the most unusual job interview, I kept my mouth shut. One week before leaving to never come back again, I started packing my bags. I also broke the news to my grandpa Toufic, and he was very happy for me. He had immigrated to Brazil, now he was seeing his favorite grandson immigrate to the United States. He could relate. He was a lot like a father to me, I get tears in my eyes just writing these words right now...

Finally, the LAST NIGHT in Brazil I went to my father's house, plugged my laptop on his big screen TV and opened up Facebook. Then I showed him all these cool guys from Kicker, riding Harley Davidson bikes, having a great time with their beautiful families and friends. He was a bit weirded out, not grasping why I was showing him that stuff. I asked him the question: "What do you think of these folks?" He said, "They look pretty cool... Why?" Then I said, "Well, these are my work colleagues now." He looked at me in SHOCK. I knew it... I knew he wouldn't want me to go.

I jumped on that freaking airplane, and arrived on March 26 in Stillwater, Oklahoma... Just a very smart and quite unhealthy Brazilian guy with nothing, NOTHING but $200 bucks in his pocket, waiting for a modest paycheck that wouldn't come for 45 days... And the rest is history.

Background

3 pages | 4 minutes

Acknowledgements

My mother not only provided me shelter for 28 years, but she paid for all my schooling and health insurance alone. Living together for as long as we did was very difficult, but each time we fought less and incentivized one another more. The last years prior to myself getting hired, we rarely had any disagreement and became supportive friends. When I was deeply troubled at the age of seven or eight, she went as far as frequently having a negative balance on her bank account to write checks for Dr. Maria Inês Giora (obrigado Tia Inês!), a phenomenal psychologist that helped me in my most difficult moments. If it wasn't for my mother I could never have ventured out as much as I did, or for as long as I did. When everything went sideways in L.A., I went back to Brazil and found shelter again in that tiny bedroom that has always been there for me. From there, once again, I was able to venture out without the concern of being unwelcome. My greatest desire for you, mother, is that you find a strong, loving and kind man, and get married again.

If it wasn't for my father, I'd be a perfect square guy, afraid to go out into the world, afraid to hit the road without a map, afraid of conflicts and standing my ground. Thank you, father, for giving me leeway to explore the world and showing that not all is bad or must be a burden. Thanks to you, I played soccer with kids from the favelas, sang a ton of Karaoke, and drank beer with badass motorcyclist friends. I still remember how the thin rain looked like liquid gold reflecting the sunrise light as we drove down the beach with the sunroof open. You taught me that life is more than doing what is supposed to be right all the time. Thank you for teaching me to never judge anyone quickly, even the ones that are marginalized by society. Thank you for teaching me humility, loving nature, and treating waitresses like best friends. I sincerely hope you find stability, get married, and live well into an old age.

Originally from Lebanon, my grandpa Toufic arrived in Brazil with nothing, and through hard work, faith and determination, built a great life. He was truly an entrepreneur, very kind, generous, and always gave a lot back to the community, especially through charity. His demeanor with others was calm, humorous, incredibly humble and soft spoken. Thank you for setting an example of work ethic, believing in me, and telling me to be patient and keep working. Thank you for waiting for me to depart from Brazil and establish myself in the U.S. before you made it to the other side. You live in my heart for eternity.

I would like to thank my friend and Freudian psychotherapist Maria Inês Giora. Thank you for picking up a call when I was panicking at 1:00 AM when I was only eight years old. Thank you for being extremely generous with your time, taking a true interest in me as a human being, and saying that one day you would hear about me for sure. If I get to help as many people as I am planning to, it will be simply paying forward the good that you've done.

I want to especially thank my friends Carllinhos Nuhá, Bernardo Chianca, Severino Xavier and Gordon Gerstheimer. You guys gave me a completely new frame of reference for what it is like to be in a TEAM.

Carllinhos, thank you for having faith in the 18 years old me full of hopes and dreams of creating the perfect audio gear for musicians. Thank you for inviting me to be a part of your life and family, and all the wonderful moments that came with it.

Severino, thank you for completely having my back, being an amazing friend, and choosing to spend your time selling my products. I miss the days we travelled together going to different audio stores in Brazil and being at the EMMA contest. Thank you for being almost uncontrollably happy for me when I got hired by Kicker after the struggle you've seen up close.

Bernardo, thank you for believing in the things I created despite knowing what the "lab" looked like in my bedroom. Thanks for helping me deal with all the customer support online, it would've been a much greater challenge without you, as I was already so overstretched.

Gordon, what can I say, my friend?! You're like family, period. Thank you for setting an example of character and all the wonderful advice you gave me. I absolutely love how you're dead serious about work, and yet, have a great sense of humor! Thank you for believing in me first and in the products that I created second. If it wasn't for you, I wouldn't have gone half as far in my professional life, and consequently, in my personal life too.

Finally, I would like to thank my great friend Steve Irby for your warm and kind friendship. Thank you for allowing me to share my difficulties with you, and for giving me wise advice and hope. If it wasn't for you, I would've left the U.S. before even having my green card, as the social relationship issues and loneliness were almost too much to bear. Even more so, I thank you for being there for me from a completely selfless standpoint, as you proved time and time again.

Fernando Eid Pires

Intro

2 pages | 3 minutes

There's no distance between you and me.

I never won the lottery. I never built and sold a company for millions of dollars. I'm not a real-estate tycoon or an expert in stock investments. I never made a salary to be proud of until April of 2021, at which point I had been in the U.S. for just five years, starting with nothing. I ate a lot of cheap cereal with milk on styrofoam plates to stretch a little bit of the dollars I had, waiting for my first paycheck.

In the beginning, people from work would see me riding my bicycle to the office in extreme Oklahoma weather and feel bad for me. I was the guy that got sick multiple times a year and needed antibiotics frequently. I'm not that guy anymore. Very rapidly, I built a GOOD life from scratch, without any major strikes of luck, shortcuts, or extraordinary accomplishments.

In fact, in just two years I already had a decent car fully paid for, an excellent credit score, and over three months worth of living expenses in my savings account—all of which was obtained on a technician's salary that many Americans can make without a degree. In less than five years and before making an excellent salary, I already had two-year's worth of savings, a credit score of 771, a duplex property in which I live on one side and rent out the other side, a truck and a sports car, and most important of all, excellent health. Not bad, right? Remember, I started with nothing but $200 bucks. No magic formula, no get rich quick scheme.

After learning how to get my life together, I wrote this very short and to the point book to help you, my friend, get your life together too. But just getting our life together is not enough, for both you and me. We need more than a good normal life to jump out of bed looking forward to the day. We need to live well today, while at the same time creating an amazing life for the future, the kind that makes

JUMPSTART

us happy and inspired, the kind that makes us glow and spread happiness wherever we go, the kind that give us a sense of purpose and an unlimited supply of hope, both of which directly impact our happiness today. For this reason, this book is not just about getting your life together, but instead, it is about getting your life together while working on your dreams of a brilliant future!

Throughout this book, keep reminding yourself that there's no distance between you and I. Remember that five years ago, I'd envy you for having any sort of car that takes you from point A to B, sheltered from the wind and the rain. Remember that much was accomplished with an "okay" salary. You have no grounds to put me on a pedestal or to say that I was lucky. It was hard work, it was discipline that gave me a good life and the knowledge to write this book in service to you, for your wellbeing. It doesn't matter how smart you think I am, the numbers don't lie, and my numbers are the same sort of numbers that you can obtain, if you too decide to get your life together.

Lastly, the keyboard key most used to type this book was the Backspace, as I would not put any extra words that don't bring value to you. For this reason, pay close attention to every sentence, as you will get knowledge, insight and usable information from every single one of them. I was told by a professional editor that if I wanted to publish this book, I would have to bulk it up. I said, "Screw it," I'm going to self-publish then. I hope this works out, as 51% of the profits goes to Doctors Without Borders.

Nice to meet you, my friend.

LET'S DO THIS!

Chapter 1

4 pages | 5 minutes

What is YOUR definition of success?

Genuine success is getting to a point in life where you are happy with yourself, what you have, and not jealous of others. "What you have" includes your relationships, circumstances, and finances.

- What you need to be successful is unique to you; success is not a one-size-fits-all.
- Genuine success can only happen through acceptance and change.
- What you overcome is just as important as what you achieve—or even more, dare I say.
- HOW you go about achieving what you desire matters the most.
- Money is the means to an end, not the end in and of itself.

Success can only happen through both acceptance and change. Think about it, if you simply *accept everything* as is, in theory, you could be happy with yourself, what you have, and not be jealous of others—meeting the criteria. The problem is that in this case, there would be no growth or progress whatsoever, both of which are key for happiness. Everyone wants to amount to something in life and that can't happen through acceptance only.

On the other hand, as much as you can change a multitude of things, from the shape of your body to your bank account and spiritual practices, you *cannot change everything*. Therefore, a change-only approach will never be *enough*. Yes, you can achieve massive growth through that, but also massive unhappiness too. I believe this to be the case with many overachievers that end up killing themselves—like Robin Williams, for example.

By no means "acceptance" means settling for less than the life you can potentially live; quite the contrary, with acceptance you can go very far, whereas denial—the opposite of acceptance—stops you dead in your tracks. The key is to use acceptance not to stop, but to begin the process of transformation for the better. Then, once the results of your transformation begin to surface, it's through acceptance that you can actually ENJOY them. By accepting such results and feeling grateful for them, you don't need to stop progressing, but rather, you can—and most likely will want to—continue to progress out of curiosity and love, finding out how far you can go while having a good time. For example, you may start a side business that you love with the goal to complement your income. Once your income is where you need it to be, you don't need to stop there; you may continue growing your business out of enjoyment, and for the good that it does to you and others.

Imagine that Jay is overweight. Denial is when he says, "I'm not fat" and does nothing about it. Transformational acceptance is when Jay says, "Yep, I'm a bit on the heavy side, so I am going to change." Once Jay is at a healthy weight—assuming that he did put in the necessary work—, another healthy form of acceptance is when Jay says, "Man, I'm so glad I've done this, I feel great!" And with that, Jay has become successful in his transformation. Does he need to stop progressing? Absolutely not. Since a healthy lifestyle has become his new normal, he might just continue to move forward and progress because he loves working out, running, hiking, etc. Now Jay is progressing out of love, and he is headed to a future of health and longevity—Jay has become successful in *this area* of his life.

Had Jay not accepted the results of his own efforts, he would probably resort to questionable supplements or illegal drugs, over-exercise, go under plastic surgeries, etc., breaking his own health by this excessive, ill-driven pursuit. In this case Jay has failed to enjoy the great results of his transformation, and he would still be jealous of others that have "that perfect body." In other words, Jay would become unsuccessful not by lack of change and progress, but by lack of acceptance.

In sum, we need acceptance to begin change, then we need acceptance to enjoy what has changed. Without acceptance, change may never happen, and when it does, no amount of change will ever be enough to make you feel happy. Moreover, for the things in life that we can't change—like your background—we have no choice but to accept it and move forward.

Also, we need to accept both *what we need* and *what we don't need,* to genuinely feel successful. Some people need to be wealthy entrepreneurs, shine on TV, and live in a big city, others need to grow their own crops, meditate, and live quietly in nature—like they say, "whatever floats your boat," my friend. Keep in mind that we only have 24 hours in a day; the time you spend going after what you *don't need,* is time lost that you could be going after what you *really need*. For example, being an employer is highly important to me, and for this reason, instead of actively looking for a higher paying job or trying to *climb the corporate ladder*, I spend a lot of time working on projects that can lead up to a full-blown business in the future.

Even more important than *what* you need, is *how* you go about obtaining it. The "what" is YOUR problem and no one else's—no judgements! Need a Ferrari? Great, work to get one! However, "HOW" does affect us all as a society; you can make the same money by trafficking drugs and exploiting people, or by creating an ethical business that offers jobs for those that need it the most—huge freaking difference. Therefore, I don't care for *what* is in your agenda, but I certainly do care about *how* you're going to pursue it. Remember that, when your head hits the pillow, you want to be *happy with yourself* in the first place! You can't hurt your brother without hurting yourself.

As we all know, there are many people that achieve high status, and yet, they don't feel happy. I believe that these people were succeeding in *achieving more* as their first priority but failing to *overcome* the issues that made them unhappy. For example, a person whose self-esteem is hurt may become rich and famous, and yet, never truly feel fulfilled—because that person needs to love him or herself first, before others do. A person who's been afraid to lose money and suddenly makes a lot of money, instead of enjoying the wealth, may become even more afraid of losing money. What I am trying to say is that overcoming your fears, traumas, and insecurities is not any less important than the house you live in and the car you drive. Genuine success is made of what you overcome AND what you achieve—not just one OR the other, it's both.

The good news is that we don't need to stop going after the material things that we desire to do healing work first, because we can work in a way that *the very road to success **is** the healing work*! When you develop better habits, give flow to your creativity, develop a healthy relationship with failure, etc., you heal on multiple levels, while working towards what you want to have. Pretty awesome, right? By practicing what I preach here, I have overcome physical, emotional, and spiritual issues. My financial life improved multifold, not at the expense, but at the expansion of my health.

Lastly, it is fundamental that we rethink money. I'd like to think of it as both a key and a lever. A key because it *unlocks* many doors; with an abundance of money, you can go anywhere in the world, experience different cultures, and most importantly, have *access* to what you need and want. A lever because you can exert a higher force; with an abundance of money, your impact—for better or worse—can be much stronger. For instance, instead of just helping yourself (a.k.a. "making a living"), you can also help a GREAT number of people! In both cases, the benefit of money is in its *usage*—provided that it is used for good. For this reason, I want to encourage you to think about what good things you'll DO with money, for yourself and others.

It is in this framework that we will move forward with each chapter; working on what you can and should change, accepting what you cannot change, understanding what you need and what you don't need, and most importantly, pursuing YOUR success in a way that uplifts others.

Chapter 2

4.5 pages | 6 minutes

Your Valuable Time

ALL we have is time. If you were to live eternally, *eventually* you would become all that you aspire to be and have all the things that you desire. However, the clock is ticking, and your best bet to become successful is to focus the use of your time on the most meaningful aspects of your life.

- Between your 20s and 30s you have the most power and leverage to create the rest of your life; be not wasteful but caring of how you spend these ten short years.
- The future will come just as fast as the past went by. It is your choice to get there accomplished or empty handed.
- The better your health, the better you can make use of your time.
- Beware of time-wasting people and social media platforms.

Because your time is limited, whenever you say 'YES' to one thing, you are saying 'NO' to another. To jumpstart your life, you absolutely need to prioritize the use of your time according to your definition of success (chapter 01). It is easy to be swayed into doing the things that *others want* us to do, or even what *we think we want* to do, just to later find ourselves deprived of the time to do what we genuinely MUST do.

Spend as much time as possible in the activities and with the people that contribute to creating what *you* call success. For example, I really enjoy martial arts, so *I think I want* to sign up for Karate classes. However, I will not consider myself any less successful if I have no martial arts skills, but I will definitely consider myself less successful if I fail to acquire an audience of young people that I can genuinely help. For this reason, I won't say 'YES' to martial arts, at the expense of spending less time writing this book and doing other work of this sort. In other words, the book is a *must have* thing, while Karate is not—clearly, Vandamme and I have different priorities! How about you, what are your *must haves*?

By the way, I would be remiss if I didn't mention that, if you don't know what to do, doing *something* is always better than doing nothing. It's okay to work a dead-end job or study something that you're not sure of, if you still have no idea of how to better spend your time; eventually, you will get clarity about it. If that is the case, think long and hard about what we discussed in chapter 1. Let's move forward assuming that you do have this clarity, or that if you don't, that you're working on it.

When you are *twenty-something*, you have tons of energy to work and can take many risks. Nothing is stopping you! If you start a company and it fails, it's ok, you're still young and "have a lot of time ahead of you." If you're in a dead-end job, you move on to the next job and "there is no hurry." Unfortunately, that is what most people think—they feel like their 20s are going to last forever, but it won't. Next thing you know, you're already past your 30s and having to think twice about your career moves. By then, you're probably looking for some financial stability, possibly getting married and having babies—if you haven't yet. As you age more, especially into your 40s, your energy to work *may* start declining, while your responsibilities surely grow.

See my point? You don't have *your whole life* to figure things out, your best bet is between the ages of 20 and 40, but even more so, the ten short years between 20 and 30. I'm not saying that it's impossible to change your life around and become successful well into your 40s and 50s, or even later. Far from it. I'm just saying that it gets HARDER. If the most precious years you have are between your 20s and your 30s, then that represents only 11% of your life—give or take. Those ten years will define how you'll get to live your next SIXTY long, remaining years; from your habits and body health, all the way up to your finances and romantic partner. From that perspective, do you still think you have time to kill? I hope this has planted a useful sense of urgency in you—be not wasteful, but considerate of your time and the time of others, my friend!

The younger you are, the greater is your *leverage* and your *willpower* to create the life that truly makes you happy. Imagine a door; think of leverage as the position in which the door handle is installed and think of willpower as the strength of the arm that is going to pull it open. There's a reason why door handles are installed on the edge of the door; because the farther out it is from the pivoting point, the higher is the leverage, and therefore, the easier it is to open it. If the same door handle were to be installed on the same door, but more inwards and closer to the pivoting point, much more effort would be required to open this door.

That's how your age works. The farther out you are from where you pivot to the other side (a.k.a. "die") the easier it is to make changes in your life. Aging is likened to the door handle moving each time farther from the edge and closer to the pivoting point of this imaginary door that represents your life. Don't wait until you lose half of your leverage to start thinking about opening the door to a fulfilling life for yourself—the sooner you start this process, the better!

Everyone thinks that their time is more valuable than anyone else's. If you have someone in your life that won't stop asking for "favors," it's time (pun not intended) to draw the line and say NO. By all means, help a friend, spend your time being useful to others, nurture the relationships that are worthwhile! Just don't let anyone abuse your time, and don't abuse theirs. It's easy to get caught up in useless meetings, pointless conversations, unnecessary drama, etc. Excuse yourself nicely and walk away—your minutes are more precious than your dollars, that's for sure. Likewise, be conscious that when you ask someone for a favor, you're asking them to give you a tiny portion of their *life* which they can't ever get back—that's a BIG deal! In business, I have the habit of always sending a thank-you gift, email or text to the people that kindly spend their time meeting with me, looking at what I have to offer. Thanks to that, I know that I can meet with them again and again. When friends help me with something, like moving or fixing a car, I buy them a nice steak dinner. Don't hesitate to show appreciation for their willingness to literally spend a piece of their life with you.

I sincerely believe that much of the difference between those that accomplish a lot in a lifetime and those that don't, is that the ones that do, tend to work and hangout with people that value time and are productive in one form or another, whereas those that don't, stick around with time wasting people. There's only so much you can do by yourself, for this reason, keep time wasters as far away as possible and associate more with those that value your time and theirs. Even for having fun you should be mindful of your time. If you're at a party and not enjoying it, leave!

Beyond that, today we have a myriad of things that simply *steal* our time. Your attention has become a *commodity* today. How many social media platforms do we have? How about on-line gaming, cat videos on YouTube, etc.? Are you kidding me?! Keep this stuff down to a minimum in your life; your social life should be, as much as possible, in person! I hope you go out with your friends, party hard, laugh hard, dance hard, and have epic memories to giggle about when you're old, instead of wasting your *spare time* scrolling away on Facebook. Your "spare time" is valuable too, do something great with it, create memories! IMHO, even driving without a destination just to listen to some music is better than being glued to your computer or phone at home.

When it comes to doing something meaningful and improving their lives, I hear a lot of people saying, "I just don't have the time for this." Often, they do have the time, but they just don't have the *energy* to put the work in. For example, you may have the time to work on a great side-hustle but feel unable to *crank it* out; even though you actually want to do something better with your time, you may just give in to "vegging out" in front of the TV because you feel so *tired all the time*. It's hard to feel motivated if you're not feeling good physically, mentally, even spiritually, and for this reason, it's of utmost importance that you nurture yourself. This is when taking good care of your body (chapters 3 and 4) and making investments into your emotional bank account (chapter 5) makes all the difference in the world. Learn to conserve and expand your energy, so you can *make use of* the time you have—especially if you work a full-time job and want to start a side-hustle (chapter 18).

Finally, let's look together into the future with the same sense of velocity that we look at the past. We seem to always be surprised about how quickly the years pass us by, and at the same time, we feel impatient about dedicating ourselves to doing something that can dramatically improve our lives in *just* a handful of years—read about gratification (chapter 15).

For example, if you think back three years ago, doesn't it feel like it was *just yesterday*? Then, why do we feel that moving forward into the future, the same three years "will take forever" when it comes to learning new skills, creating relationships, improving your health, building-up some savings, etc.? Keep in mind that <u>working on your future makes your present better</u>, as you *immediately* feel more optimistic and in control of things. If the last three years flew by, then the next three years will also be gone before you know it—it's your choice to get there empty handed, or well accomplished. Take your pick.

Recommended Watch: <u>In Time (2011)</u>
1h 49min | Action, Sci-Fi, Thriller

Chapter 3

5 pages | 6 minutes

Your Body Temple

If you had the choice to stop at a gas station and fill up your car with junk gas, adulterated with chemicals that would lead to an immediate loss of power and possibly an expensive repair bill, would you do that? Probably not. So why do people keep eating junk food? It leads to an immediate change in mood and sometimes a big medical bill, if not permanent damage—like diabetes. If you wouldn't do that to a car, why would you do it to yourself?

- You can't be happy and enjoy life if you are sick.
- The best health care is eating well and exercising enough.
- Your health and wellbeing always come first.
- Lower GI foods are better for your health, stay away from excess sugar.
- Improving your insulin sensitivity is key for longevity and good health
- Real food doesn't have a marketing name. If it has a marketing name, it's probably not good for you.

Your body is your temple. It is much more of a house than the roof over your head; it is where your consciousness lives. Out of everything you own, your body is the most precious possession and needs the best care, and yet, it's usually taken for granted. It is so beautiful and perfect in its divine engineering, that most often we don't even contemplate how blessed we are to have a healthy and functioning body—until we don't. How are we supposed to treat a temple? With care, respect, even reverence.

You probably still have many years to live; that can be a blessing or a curse, depending on the state of your health. In modern day society, food has been turned into a form of reward, rather than a form of nurturing. They sell *tasty sugary greasy stuff* for people to reward themselves with *yumminess*—it's addictive.

Food products such as energy drinks, soda/pop, potato chips, and candy bars, are simply manmade chemicals that make you quickly addicted, and later, sick. As a result, you may spend your money feeding the medical drug industry. Diabetes kills many more people than terrorism does: in 2019, an estimated 1.5 million deaths were directly caused by diabetes, versus 28,082 by terrorism. Actual food is engineered by mother nature, not by man; if something has a marketing name to it, then it's probably not good for you—with very few exceptions.

Food has three tastes: 1- how it feels in your mouth, 2- how it feels during digestion and the immediate impact on your energy levels, and 3- how it makes you feel long-term and the impact on your health. Most food of the Standard American Diet (SAD) score high at taste #1, and horribly at tastes #2 and #3.

Before consuming food products, ask yourself, "How does it score in tastes #2 and #3?" Then you will know whether you will be honoring your Body Temple or not. Think long term! The highly inflammatory SAD contributes to depression, ADHD, increased anxiety and mood swings, lower cognitive performance, and even early onset of mental diseases such as Parkinson's and Alzheimer's. Needless to say, this gets in the way of jumpstarting your life; a cleaner diet makes for a sharper mind and a more energetic body—and you will need it.

The good news is that it doesn't take much to be healthy. Simply eliminating the junk food from your diet and including enough exercise will do the trick. For example, you can start by cutting soda/pop and candy from your diet and exercising or walking 30 minutes most days. Sweeteners, although very low in calories, have been shown to alter your gut flora in such a way that may make you gain weight and negatively affect your overall health—so it is best to avoid those as well (see #1). Stevia appears to be safe, and it is a good idea to check the scientific literature on any new sweetener products that come out before making your decision to use them.

As far as exercise is concerned, in "motivational" books, recent literature often suggests *"Beast-Mode."* That means going to the gym and overworking yourself with the heaviest of weights and pushing yourself beyond imaginable limits. I did that and don't regret it. In a way, it worked, as doing *hard things* can really build your confidence. However, I had days that I crushed myself so hard that I got sick later. I do have reservations about recommending it, therefore. Although it may work for some people, perhaps it's not what you want in order to jumpstart your life. The more brutal your workout is, the more recovery you'll need. Consequently, you need to eat and sleep more. If you want to make the most out of your day, you probably don't want to spend a lot of energy digesting copious amounts of meat and sleeping significantly more than 8 hours per night. With a moderately intense workout, you will stay healthy and in shape, but won't need to eat and sleep disproportionally more—you'll probably feel better, be more productive, and enjoy an enduring sense of balance that way. For me, the sweet spot is about 45 minutes of weightlifting four times a week and running 5 kilometers about once a week. I can cope with this amount of exercise really well, without having to eat and sleep too much. You will have to find what your balanced point is.

Beyond that, have you noticed that when you're in good spirits, you don't need to sleep as much? Being in a state of joy also lowers your need for sleep. The trouble is, it's HARD to feel joyful and happy if you're sleep deprived. For me, about seven hours of sleep works great, so long as I am consistent with my schedule. Some people do well with six, others need the whole eight hours, or more. Once you adjust your diet and exercise, you can discover what is the minimum amount of sleep that you need to perform at your best. If you have a 9-to-5 job (chapter 19) and a side-hustle (chapter 18), by sleeping six hours per night as opposed to eight, you get another two hours every day. Add that up, and you're looking at 700 more hours to work on your dreams each year! That is a LOT! I'm not suggesting for you to be sleep deprived, far from it, but I am suggesting optimizing your diet and exercise in a way that, if you're lucky, you may find you do well with a little less sleep than the usual. As always, confirm with a doctor before and during any major changes.

Food has what we call a Glycemic Index (GI); a high GI means that the sugar in it gets absorbed very quickly by your body, a low GI means a slower and buffered sugar absorption—which is much better. Food and drinks with high GI such as soda, candy, sweet juices, white bread, and sugary cereals cause a very rapid increase of your blood sugar. In response to that, your body spikes the release of insulin to control this peaking sugar level, and consequently, you experience a sugar crash later—feeling a bit lousy. It affects your mood, and of course, doesn't help your productivity.

By constantly eating high GI foods, your cells gradually become insulin resistant, which is the main reason why a person develops diabetes type II. If you want to have steady energy levels throughout the day and not become diabetic, stay away from high GI foods. For example, instead of eating Corn Flakes, you could try rolled oats instead! Look up the GI of the foods you're eating, flag the high GI ones, and replace them with a lower GI counterpart.

As far as fat goes, there is a lot of controversy. The fact is that you NEED fat to produce hormones and keep a healthy brain. Each neuron has a fat coating called the myelin sheath that prevents it from short circuiting and making undesired electrical connections left and right. Needing fat for proper health is NOT an excuse to eat fatty foods loaded with sugar, such as ice-cream. Those are the worst! But nothing is wrong with fatty foods such as walnuts, avocados, salmon, flax seeds, and olive oil. Healthy fats like these improve your brain health and function and buffer the sugar absorption of other foods, lowering the overall GI of the meal—which is a good thing.

Your insulin sensitivity is a determining factor for developing diabetes type II, as well as a myriad of other diseases. Studies show that even breast cancer is more prevalent in people with low insulin sensitivity (see #2). In other words, to prevent or delay the onset of life threatening diseases, improving your insulin sensitivity is key.

One very easy change to implement that can have a huge positive impact, is simply changing your breakfast to drop its GI level to a very low level. For example, if you had tacos (moderate GI) for dinner at 9:00 PM, then had eggs, toast and fruit juice (high GI) for breakfast at 7:30 AM, your body released considerable amounts of insulin twice in less than 12 hours. That is very typical, and of course, not helpful if you're trying to reset or improve your insulin sensitivity. However, simply swapping out the toast for avocados and the juice for unsweetened almond milk, tea or coffee, would drastically drop the GI of your breakfast to nearly zero, thus allowing you to be "insulin fasted" until the next meal, which is probably lunch. Allowing your body to rest from producing insulin for 12 or more hours every day can be wonderfully helpful. It's a simple change that can make a world of difference in avoiding, staving off or even recovering from diabetes and other insulin related diseases.

<u>The keto diet</u>: Today, there's a big hype about it. In my experience, it is a corrective diet. Unless you're on the verge of developing diabetes and you need to lower your insulin resistance as soon as possible, you may want to stay away from it. Removing ALL the carbs and ALL the sugars from your diet adds to your stress. Also, with the amount of fat recommended by the Keto Diet, your liver may be overloaded. In most cases you can lose weight and fix your diet without resorting to keto.

A sharp mind is always your safety net, especially when times are difficult. For this reason, staying away from drugs and excess alcohol is important. Of course, beer with friends, wine with your loved one, all of these are wonderful experiences, just remember to do it in moderation and always honor your body temple, my friend!

References:

1. Effects of Sweeteners on the Gut Microbiota: A Review of Experimental Studies and Clinical Trials:
   https://www.ncbi.nlm.nih.gov/pmc/articles/PMC6363527/

2. Metabolic Health, Insulin, and Breast Cancer: Why Oncologists Should Care About Insulin:
   https://www.ncbi.nlm.nih.gov/pmc/articles/PMC7045050/

Chapter 4

7 pages | 9 minutes

Physical Energy

Physical Energy (PHE) is the "get up and go," the disposition to do things without hesitation. It's getting through the day, owning your To Do list, and still feeling like you've got some juice left.

- Your PHE depends on what you EAT, THINK, and DO.
- Good digestion is just as important as a good diet.
- Stay away from questionable supplement brands.
- Use probiotics before, after and during antibiotic treatment.
- Your hormones are influenced by what you do, as well as your social environment.

You simply can't do stuff if your body refuses to. Whether you're writing an e-mail or weightlifting, it helps to be wide awake and feeling good to do it well.

I wish it was as simple as "eat the right things and feel great." It's not. Just as much as what we eat influences our PHE levels, so does what we think and what we do. Even if you eat only the best foods, thinking mostly negative thoughts and sitting around the house will make your PHE levels hit rock bottom anyway. Without question, your nutrition, hormones, and metabolism make a huge difference; but so, do other less tangible factors. For example, the thoughts of frustration with a certain situation, or anger towards someone can simply destroy my physical energy level and make you literally feel sick, even in perfect health—but we'll talk more about that in the next chapter about your Emotional Bank Account.

If you feel drained way too often without a predominantly negative mind, consult your doctor and get a detailed checkup. Look for problems with hormones, thyroid, heavy metal contamination, levels of vitamins and minerals. I'm not a doctor, but I've struggled with very low PHE levels and learned a few things that I'd like to share. <u>For your safety, consult and validate with your physician the suggestions of this chapter before implementing them.</u>

<u>Digestion</u>: If you have any sort of digestive issues, I strongly recommend you consult with a gastroenterologist as soon as possible. Fixing your digestion can improve your PHE levels and potentially make other seemingly unrelated health problems disappear, simply by more efficiently getting the nutrients from the food you eat. It's worth mentioning that digestive issues, especially gastritis and acid reflux, are often caused by emotional distress. In my case, a change of life was better than any medical treatment.

Many people have nutrient malabsorption, which, when undiagnosed, can make it such that even eating the best foods will not help them much. The first and easiest way to improve your digestion and nutrient absorption, is simply chewing your food thoroughly.

Other examples of contributing factors to nutrient malabsorption are leaky gut, unbalanced intestine bacterial flora, worms, bariatric surgery, etc. Some of these factors can be addressed, while others can be compensated for. For instance, you can take probiotics to improve your gut flora, and in the case of a bariatric surgery, you can take supplements to compensate for the difficulty in absorbing certain vitamins and minerals.

According to the recommendation of my gastroenterologist, L-Glutamine contributes to sealing the intestinal lining; leaky gut has been linked to food allergies, fatigue, and even cognitive disorders. It may be worth a try if you have food allergies, for example.

I've found that ginger helped me digest food faster and better. My stomach is pretty sensitive, especially with heavy foods with strong condiments. Whenever I'm having a digestive challenge, I make myself a ginger tea, and found it to work great to empty my stomach and process what seems to be stuck in it.

I've had acid reflux from the age of 10 until the age of 30. I could not go two days without Proton Pump Inhibitors (PPI), or I'd be spitting out fire. I changed my diet and found the best outlet for my emotional charge in weightlifting. I also used lots of ginger, cut most

JUMPSTART

of the alcohol, and avoided fried foods altogether. By the age of 33, these digestion issues became a thing of the past.

<u>Metabolic disorders</u>: From your bodyweight to your state-of-mind, your metabolism plays a key role; when too fast, you lose weight, become anxious, have trouble sleeping, become emotionally reactive, etc. When too slow, you gain weight, feel tired and unmotivated, sleep too much, etc. If you find yourself at either extreme, consult doctors specializing in metabolic disorders. If your thyroid function is not great, get yourself tested for TSH, T3 and T4 hormones. I'd recommend eating more foods rich in iodine and selenium—it may not fix it, but it can help. Ginger and Cayenne pepper are also known to boost the metabolism—just don't expect any miracles.

<u>Vitamins & Minerals</u>: Minerals are often overlooked and are just as important as vitamins—maybe even more. Low iron causes anemia, which causes fatigue. Introduce iron rich foods in your diet. Magnesium is key for many metabolic processes: strong bones, healthy blood pressure, absorption of other minerals, and even diabetes prevention. Include magnesium rich foods in your diet. You might also consider a magnesium supplement. If you have constipation, give a good magnesium supplement a shot; it's great for that. However, magnesium overdose causes diarrhea.

Vitamin D: Your immune system, cancer fighting ability, bone density, and even mood regulation is highly dependent on your vitamin D levels. There is a worldwide epidemic of low vitamin D because most people don't get enough sun. The required sun exposure for optimal Vitamin D levels will depend on your geographic location, percentage of skin exposure, and exposure time. For most people, it's not quite feasible or convenient to get a sufficient amount of sun. Also, sun exposure does come with the downside of increasing the likelihood of developing skin cancer. For these reasons, Vitamin D supplementation can be very beneficial.

The normal range of vitamin D in your blood is between 30 to 100 ng/mL. I weigh 165lbs and by using 5000 IU daily, my labs show 56 ng/mL—which is right on target. Since vitamin D is fat soluble, for better absorption, take it with fatty foods such as avocados, eggs, or olive oil.

Omega-3: You won't feel an "energy boost" by taking it, and the results are subtle and slow to show. However, the way it works is that the Omega-3 becomes part of the membrane of your cells, and as a consequence, powerful anti-inflammatory compounds are produced. Having low inflammation in your body has system-wide benefits, from healthier joints and better immune response to brain health. A word of caution: Omega-3 supplements must come from a reputable brand, as low quality or contaminated fish oil can be dangerous to your health. Either get the good stuff, or don't get it at all.

B vitamins: These are extremely beneficial for your brain health, metabolism, digestion, and energy production. Particularly, B12 helps prevent anemia and is very beneficial for your brain, even preventing or delaying the onset of mental diseases such as Alzheimer's. Ideally, you want to get your blood tested for B vitamin deficiencies before you supplement. However, the B vitamins are water soluble, so you are unlikely to have any signs of toxicity from them. You can always try a B complex and see how you feel. If you have no improvements, that's good news. If your PHE level is dramatically improved, maybe your body has trouble absorbing them from food, and supplementing may come in handy. In the beginning of my journey in improving my fragile health, taking a Vitamin B complex made all the difference, it was like night and day. As my health got better and my vitamin levels became adequate, taking or not taking a B complex made no difference—which is a good sign.

Gut Bacteria: Our immune system, mood, and nutrition levels are highly dependent on the bacterial flora in our gut. For example, it influences our dopamine and vitamin K2 levels. Having the habit of regularly ingesting probiotic foods, such as kefir, kombucha, and unsweetened organic yogurt, are a good way to keep your good bugs nourished. Sometimes it may be necessary to use a quality probiotic supplement—in the event of diarrhea or antibiotic treatment. Antibiotics will literally kill off your beneficial gut bacteria; they change your gut flora with the first pill! <u>Always take a probiotic supplement before, during, and after antibiotic treatment</u>.

Worms: If you haven't been treated for them in years, there's a good chance that you're feeding a family rather than just yourself.

JUMPSTART

Worms can cause anemia and vitamin deficiencies. If you can afford it, consult a doctor for proper exams and treatment.

<u>Hormonal Balance:</u> Not only what you eat, but what you DO and your social environment, play a role in your hormonal balance; as much as possible, adjust these other two factors to contribute to your hormonal health.

Cortisol: Known as the "stress hormone," it makes you get up and get going in the morning. Too little of it, and you'll find it hard to get out of the bed and may feel sluggish throughout the day. When too high, it causes immune system suppression, tissue breakdown, and edginess! You want it high in the morning and low at night. A stressful social environment, like a workplace where people are trying to pull the rug from under you, keeps your cortisol levels high throughout the day. That can make you seriously sick over time and change the levels of other hormones, causing problematic imbalances. Exercising regularly and moderately causes the body to adapt better to stress, reducing cortisol output over time; consequently, you can better handle stressful situations in life. For example, working out can make you more relaxed when getting cut off in traffic and dealing with a difficult coworker! Always nourish your body before and after your workout to prevent excess amounts of cortisol—please, don't go to the gym hungry.

Endorphins: These are pain-relievers and happiness boosters. If you're feeling a little down, you can chemically improve your mood with an intense exercise session that lasts long enough (10 to 30 minutes) to release endorphins. The "runner's high" is caused by endorphin release. When I am too much in my head, obsessing about something, I go out for a run that lasts at least 30 minutes, and usually that calms me down quite a bit. Endorphins are the reason why people that exercise regularly are usually happy, and also the reason why many athletes get depressed after an injury, as they become unable to reach their normal levels of endorphins from exercise. It's very powerful.

Dopamine: This chemical is mostly known for being the reward hormone. The body releases healthy amounts when solving problems and challenges. It gives you euphoria, bliss, motivation, and concentration. It feels awesome! Foods rich in L-Tyrosine, such as dairy, eggs, almonds, and walnuts help your body produce dopamine. This same hormone can make us addicted to detrimental habits such as gambling. However, when you focus on the right activities, it buffers the stress and keeps you motivated.

Testosterone: Both men and women experience sluggishness, lack of motivation, and low libido when testosterone is low. Cortisol decreases testosterone, so managing stress is important to keep it at an optimal level. There's also evidence that low-fat diets decrease testosterone; a diet rich in good fats is more appropriate to support a healthy production of testosterone. Studies (see 1) show that compound exercises, which work multiple muscle groups at the same time, such as deadlifts and squats increase the level of testosterone. Long cardio activities (such as running for over an hour) may lower it.

Oxytocin: You may know this neurotransmitter as "the love hormone." Human contact, such as sex, hugs or even a simple handshake, causes a healthy release of oxytocin. It makes you relaxed, gives a sense of belonging, and raises your stress tolerance, which in turn, reduces cortisol. Go ahead and hug your friends, pet your dog and hi-five complete strangers!

Your body is a complex mechanism and information on how to take care of it can be overwhelming. Instead of feeling hopeless about not knowing how to do it all perfectly, take it one step at a time and seek the guidance of your doctor. To further simplify, taking a Vitamin D supplement is a necessity for nearly everyone. Provided that your digestion and diet is good, you probably don't need anything else. Personally, I take Vitamin D in the morning, along with a reputable food-based multivitamin supplement. Stay away from unknown supplement brands, especially those that promise to boost everything in your life. Because supplements are not regulated by the FDA, you can be taking a placebo or even something harmful—there's a LOT of scams in the supplement industry.

References:

1. 5 moves to boost your testosterone
   https://www.menshealth.com/uk/building-muscle/a757409/5-moves-to-boost-your-testosterone/

Chapter 5

6 pages | 7 minutes

Your Emotional Bank Account

You essentially have two bank accounts: a financial bank account (FBA) and an emotional bank account (EBA). If both have low balances, the first one that needs to be improved is your EBA.

- A healthy EBA makes you more energetic, happy and driven to pursue the changes to improve your FBA
- Your physical health is directly related to your EBA.
- Feeling apathetic is often confused with feeling tired. These are different problems with different solutions.
- Forgiving the ones that hurt you is not for their sake, but for yours.

Have you seen those people who always seem to be happy, that can do 10 different things in a day and never feel tired? Even I envy them sometimes! It's through a wealthy EBA that they achieve that *life force*. There's nothing more helpful than a great EBA to feel happy and work on your dreams with grit. Not only do these people have a great time grinding out work, but they're often healthier and more successful. If your physical health is fine but you feel like you've been run over by a bulldozer at the end of the day, chances are, your EBA balance is low. If your EBA balance goes negative, you can feel down, fatigued, depressed, and even angry. A low EBA can also manifest physically: for example, producing a weak immune system or an upset stomach.

The good news is that you can make deposits to your EBA starting TODAY, and to do so, it only requires your awareness and commitment. Like any bank account, the key is to have more deposits than withdrawals or leaks.

A series of *dos and don'ts* will follow, but keep in mind that you can only accomplish so much at a time. To avoid becoming frustrated, take reasonable steps instead of trying to accomplish all of them at once. Praise yourself for what you can do and forgive yourself for what you cannot. With that in mind:

A *Withdrawal* is when you consciously take some of your emotional energy out to invest it in someone, like a friend or a romantic partner, or something, like a fulfilling hobby, a side hustle, charity work, etc. These are great emotional energy investments because they are likely to give you positive returns, thus further improving your EBA.

A *Leak* is when you *lose* some of your emotional energy by accident or without your intention. Examples of leaks include having to interact with negative people, keeping a disorganized house, criticizing yourself and others too much, etc.

After engaging in an activity, going out somewhere, or interacting with a person or group of people, ask yourself: How do I feel? If you feel tired, like you have a little *less life in you*, then it was a leak. If you feel vibrant, *wanting more*, then it was a deposit! Bring this awareness to your life, in order to select more wisely the places you go and the people you hang out with. Keep in mind that leaks are part of life too and that's fine—worrying too much about these leaks is a leak in itself.

Fixing the Leaks: Distance yourself from negative people as much as conveniently possible, especially those that like to complain about everything: the government, their boss, society, the price of things, etc. For example, if in a group of friends there's someone who is a complainer, say Hi, talk a little bit, just don't spend the majority of your time with that particular person. This also means quitting the political wars on social media and the upsetting videos on YouTube.

JUMPSTART

For those from whom you can't distance yourself, like negative coworkers and family members, learn to coexist with them without getting pulled into what they say. If they approach you and start a conversation, be polite but don't engage—misery loves company! They are usually eager to impose on others *their* pessimistic version of "reality," but you don't have to buy into what they say. If you don't engage with them, they will probably no longer reach out to you, and you're not going to miss that.

Keep up with the required maintenance in life: dishes in the sink, a dirty car, a messy work desk, a messy house, any sort of loose ends like that are a source of leakage and discontentment. Keep those nice and tidy, but without obsessing about it.

Never spend time and energy on problems that you can't fix; instead, worry about what you can actually change for the better—your life, especially. Really, what's the point of getting all worked up about something that you can't mend, improve, touch, or influence? Knowing what is going on in your country and in the world is a good thing, but obsessing about it is not. If you find yourself having strong emotions from watching the news, I suggest that you reduce or temporarily quit watching it. In large, newscasters present very negative content that you can't do anything about. It is okay for you to take a break from it and focus on yourself, especially if your goal is to become a more positive and happier individual.

Love more, hate less. Do you hate your ex, the president, your boss, or even a certain media personality? Hating is not a leak; it's a toilet flush! When someone that you *hate* comes to mind, ask yourself, "If I wasn't thinking about this person, what would I be thinking about instead?" Then switch over to that thought. I too sometimes catch myself getting all worked up about someone I don't like, but then I just ask myself, "What would I be thinking about instead, if I wasn't wasting my time and spirit thinking about this person?" and the answer usually is something that I have to do, or even better, something about a project that I enjoy doing; then I simply steer my mind to that direction and keep it there.

FORGIVE those that have hurt you. When you forgive someone, it does NOT mean that you accept or approve their behavior. You just *let go* of them, releasing that hate and judgement towards them. The truth is that we never know what happened to someone in the past, and why they do what they do. For example, I know someone who lies through his teeth and is extremely narcissistic. It just bothers me to be anywhere near the guy—big leak. But knowing a little better, I understand that something really bad must have happened to him during his upbringing to result in that kind of behavior. I feel sorry that he never overcame that! Do I approve his behavior? NO, absolutely not. But I forgive him, I let him go. Obviously, at the same time that you forgive someone like that, you can and should still protect yourself from future "jabs" that this particular person may try to inflict on you. If that person has hurt you before, set your boundaries and keep an eye out, so that person can't hurt you again. Like I said, forgiving doesn't mean approving, let alone making yourself vulnerable and wide open to future attacks. Forgiving means *releasing*. When you don't forgive, you're not holding burning coals over that person's head, but instead, you have coals burning inside of you. You are hurting YOU, not them. Forgive them not for their sake, but for yours. A good expression to keep in mind is: "Holding onto anger is like drinking poison and expecting the other person to die."

Other severe leakage sources are negative self-talk, lying to others, revenge, procrastinating, indecision, and addictions (drugs, alcohol, porn, social media, etc.). All of these can be mitigated or eliminated by *creating better habits and committing to live with integrity*—more on that in the next chapter about Self-Esteem.

Making Investments: Habits are either the biggest contribution or the biggest drainage to your EBA. Break the habits that are a leakage to your EBA, and in place, form habits (chapter 09) that support it.

Get closer to vibrant people, especially those that you admire and have some personality traits that you would like to have yourself. This can be done mentally, simply by paying less attention to negative people and more attention to vibrant and inspiring people. Chances

JUMPSTART

are that you can't magically surround yourself with the coolest, most inspiring humans, but you can definitely re-direct your focus. If you can't find anyone wise and vibrant around you, you can find and follow them on YouTube, Instagram, etc. For example, I love to follow Will Smith, I find him to be a really cool and humble guy, and he has never failed to inspire me! Often, when I need a "pick me up," I type up his name on YouTube and listen to some of his motivational material.

Calibrate your self-talk. We all have a voice inside of us, sometimes it is kind and encouraging, sometimes it is harsh and puts us down. The first thing is understanding that this voice is *in you,* but it is *not* you. Create the habit to observe and question this voice, by doing that on a regular basis, you become more aware of whether this voice is being reasonable and fair, or if it is working against you. Your goal is to *be your* own *best friend.* And what is it that best friends do? First, they encourage us to do what is in our best interest and praise us for doing well. But also, they call us out when we're making bad decisions, and they incentivize us to get out of a funk.

Appreciate self-doubt. We all have a little voice inside of us that says we are not enough, or cannot do something, don't we? The difference is what you **choose** to do with it. Self-doubt is the most wonderful sign that you are exactly where you should be—about to push yourself. Use it not to stop, but to fuel you! I, too, have this little voice in me, but I'm grateful for it, for every time I heard this little voice of doubt, I became more determined to prove it wrong. The more doubt I had, the harder I worked! I would say that the most impressive things I've done and created were the result of me overcompensating for my own self-doubt. Next time you have self doubt, just remind yourself that you're just facing a challenge, and that's a good thing. The more you overcome such challenges, the less susceptible you become to negative self-talk and the more you will appreciate self-doubt.

Find the work that you're NOT doing that would energize you. This may sound counterintuitive—how come having more work to do will help with my EBA? It's simple, your EBA is highly dependent on how much fulfillment you have in life. You can get a lot of motivation by doing work that you love. This is especially true if you don't have the fulfillment you need at your job. This could be drawing, painting, playing an instrument, volunteering, gardening, working out, etc. Doing something that you *care* about and love, has the potential to make you happier and less "tired" than NOT doing it. The quote marks on "tired" are intentional, because we often confuse feeling *apathetic*, with feeling tired. If you want to curb this apathy, doing exciting, purposeful, fulfilling work is a sure way.

Create a *happy morning ritual*. Start your day by supporting your EBA with a productive activity that you love, as mentioned above. Choosing an activity with potential financial gain is even better, which is the reason why I recommend working on your side hustle (chapter 18) first thing in the morning. If you *make* your morning great, you can't have an *all-bad* day ever—even if shit hits the fan later in the day! It's as simple as that. In the long run, this will have a huge positive impact on your EBA.

Practice gratitude. Ask yourself, "What is it that I have, which if I lose and get back, would make me extremely happy?" Your health? Your functioning brain? Your roof? Your car? Clean air? Your job? Food? Family and those who care about you? Gratitude is the feeling that is the most EBA-supportive. Try exercising gratitude with what you have and welcoming more. If you pray, you can always say, "Thank you for my good health. Thank you for all the material and financial resources that allow me to live and work to help myself and others." Even if you're making minimum wage, remember that you are *crazy rich* compared to most people in poor countries, who may not even have clean water to drink and proper sewage service.

Lastly, I strongly encourage you to have a spiritual practice daily. Whether you're religious or not, spiritual practices are a sure way to fill up your EBA. They may include taking a meditative walk in the park, praying to a higher power, practicing yoga, or simply sitting in silence for a few minutes. The most resilient, happy, and wealthy

JUMPSTART

people I know are diligent in their spiritual practices. Take a moment and give a gift to yourself by acquiring a spiritual habit—it's worth it.

Chapter 6

6 pages | 7 minutes

Self Esteem

"Money, success, fame, all that stuff is irrelevant, what matters is what you think about yourself, when you're by yourself"—Tom Bilyeu. More than ever, today we're tempted to pursue *external success* more than *internal success*. You don't have to choose one OR the other, but if you want to be *happy*, your internal success (a.k.a. "self-esteem") must be your top priority, and your external success (a.k.a. "status"), a *result*.

- Healthy self-esteem contributes to your success, happiness and even physical wellness.
- Self-esteem works as an emotional immune system, allowing you to take more risks, benefit from failures and criticism without emotional damage.
- You can only have good self-esteem if you live in integrity.
- Self-esteem is the reputation that you acquire with yourself; by doing the *hard things* that are good for you and others, you improve this "reputation."

In simple terms, *success* is simply a group of positive outcomes in multiple areas of your life, including relationships, health, and finances. If you are on *autopilot*, living without awareness, <u>your decisions, actions and habits are only as good as your self-esteem</u>—all of which have a huge impact on such outcomes. In other words, normally the quality of your life is proportional to the health of your self-esteem, and vice-versa. Because of the *interdependence* between the quality of your life and the health of your self-esteem, when YOU are *proactive* about improving your life, your self-esteem improves. For example, if you transition from a life in which you smoke, don't exercise, and have messy finances, into a life that you work-out regularly, are tobacco free, and have organized finances, your self-esteem will improve. Once your self-esteem is improved, you will *want* to keep this healthier lifestyle, because you feel that you *deserve it*—but to make the initial transition, you'll need to commit and push yourself to do it.

So, is self-esteem the result of a good life? Well, no. If someone just came by and *gave you* a better life, your self-esteem wouldn't get any better; because it's not the good life per se that leads up to a good self-esteem, but it is the merit, the effort, and the hard things that you need to DO to create a good life that does it. That's why there is no shortage of "spoiled kids" with existential crises and self-esteem problems—because they never had to *do the hard things* to create such a good life. In fact, it's not uncommon to see people win the lottery and *self-sabotage* right back into the hard life they truly feel deserving of, effectively losing everything. People with good self-esteem not only don't let their lives move backwards, but they're also very motivated to make it great—and keep it that way.

When you take ownership of your life and take improvements into your own hands, every little proof of progress is a milestone to the health of your self-esteem—even things as simple as making the bed every morning without fail. As your self-esteem gets better and better, you will *naturally* act in a way that brings about genuine success. For this reason, working on your self-esteem is not an inconvenience, but an accelerator to a truly good life.

Not under any circumstance whatsoever, can anyone possibly have good self-esteem unless they choose to live in integrity. Living in integrity is by far the best choice you can make for yourself, and it is a lot more than simply telling the truth. Here are a few examples of less obvious things that you have to *avoid* in order to live in integrity: omitting or stretching the truth, pretending to be happy when you're not (the "always nice" person), pretending to be sad when you're not (the manipulative person), pretending to care when you don't (and vice-versa), praising when you don't mean it (a.k.a. "B.S.ing"), being dismissive when you're impressed (jealousy), taking credit for someone else's work, transferring responsibility, not admitting fault, always being late, blowing off commitments with yourself and others, underselling or overselling your talents and abilities, failing to admit to yourself who you really are and what you really want, staying in a job or relationship that your heart has moved on from, etc. Watch School Ties (1992) and observe how David Greene keeps his integrity, and how that affects how he sees himself, as well as how others see him.

    Let's say that Kyle doesn't think too highly of himself, and for this reason, he feels the necessity to overcompensate with power and status in order to feel that he has value as a person. Because of this hole in his soul, he is willing to get that external validation at any cost. By deceit, he gets to climb the corporate ladder and make his way to the top, by taking credit for other people's work, abusing others, "kissing up," and telling lies that make him look good. Well, at that point he might have all the external success he wants, but deep inside, he only aggravated his own poor self-image. Behind the wheel of that fancy car, stands a guy whose reputation with himself is poor. Kyle will never, ever be a happy person that way—that is the *worst* possible failure, my friend. If you take everything away from Kyle, he will be left with nothing but his poor opinion of himself.

    However, let's imagine that Kyle realized that he ended up even more unhappy by pursuing external success in such a deplorable way, so he went back in time and decided to do things differently. Kyle then, made sure he always kept his word, cherished the success of others, and he stood by the truth even when it seemed to hurt his own interests. He ferociously pursued external success through great work ethic (chapter 13) and without compromising morality and integrity. As a result, not only did he obtain all the nice things he craved but also the admiration of others. Moreover, he healed his heart and soul in the

JUMPSTART

process. Kyle's reputation with himself (a.k.a. self-esteem) is now stellar. Even if you take everything away from Kyle, you can't take away his dignity!

Once you choose to live in integrity, you can improve your self-esteem by *doing hard things*. If you are in a difficult place in your life, this may be ridding yourself from addictions, paying off debts, etc. If you're past that (or have never been there in the first place), there's no shortage of good *hard things* you can do that will actually get you closer to your goals and success; for example, learning new skills such as public speaking, coding, writing, speaking a new language, etc., or in the wellness realm, <u>correcting your posture</u>, running, weightlifting, cycling, dieting, etc. For this reason, rather than doing anything that may be hard but not so useful, you're better off spending your time (chapter 2) doing something hard that will have a direct and measurable positive impact in your personal and professional life, thus effectively moving you towards your goals.

Your self-esteem works as an emotional immune system that makes you much more resilient to deal with criticism (chapter 12) and failures (chapter 11); the same adversities that would crush someone with self-esteem issues, would only hurt the healthy individual to a certain point, from which he or she is able to bounce back and grow stronger. When this emotional immune system is well, you get to *play offense* in life. You can show up for the battles without a paralyzing fear of failure, which allows you to learn new skills and pursue your dreams. If you lose the battle, it's going to hurt, but it won't hurt *you*. However, when your self-esteem is not well cultivated, most likely you will get stuck *playing defense* and not going very far, trying to protect yourself at all times from criticism and failures, effectively becoming your own limiting factor.

Just like the mind has an influence on your body, so does your body have an influence on your mind. For this reason, it's important to correct your posture. Take a good, hard look in the mirror and check your posture for shoulders rolling forward and pelvic tilting—those are the most common issues with sitting all day. You may need to get professional help for correcting your posture, but you can start by searching YouTube for "shoulders rolled forward fix" and "anterior pelvic tilt fix." Most of these exercises can be done at home. Regardless of how your posture affects your self-esteem, fixing it is a really smart move to avoid future pains and growing older with spine and joint issues.

Eliminate habits that damage your self-image and replace them with new habits (chapter 09) that build it instead. For example, the habit of always being "just a couple of minutes late" for everything may not seem like a big deal, but it may create the self-image of "I am the kind of person that is always late." Not good. Set your clocks 15 minutes in advance and you'll never be late again! Other examples of habits that build your self-image are: Making the bed every morning, dealing with problems "head on," finishing everything that you started, doing better work than asked for, exercising regularly, and keeping your house and your car clean. These are simple things that cost nothing, and yet, they influence how you see yourself. Of course, each person is affected differently, you may never make your bed and always be a few minutes late for everything, and yet, have great self-esteem; but it would be fair to say that these small things can help someone that is not there yet. Examples of other damaging habits to avoid: sleeping late because of watching TV, delaying an overdue haircut, not taking care of personal hygiene regularly, wearing worn out clothes frequently, secretly watching pornography, dating the "wrong kind of people," and hanging out with people that indulge in self-pity. None of those help.

Self-talk also plays a VERY strong role in your self-esteem and ability to achieve what you want in life. When voices inside your head say, "I don't deserve this," "I can't do this," or "I can't learn that," ask these voices to give you *the reasons* why not. Many times, there will be NO good reason. In case there *is* a good reason, challenge this voice by advocating in *favor* of yourself, then *go do what it takes* to prove this voice wrong. For example, not too long ago while driving in nicer neighborhoods, I would look at those cute houses and feel that they were really out of reach. When I felt that way, I would dig deep and ask myself "Why is that?" In response, I would then think: "I am physically and mentally fit, I'm willing to learn and work more than most people, therefore I see no impediment in having a nice house such as that one." Today I own a property that I didn't think was possible for me a few years ago.

Challenge your negative self-talk and feelings of being *undeserving* by having that conversation with yourself and really *having your back*. When it comes to finding a wonderful romantic partner (chapter 26) and creating a beautiful relationship, this method of challenging your negative self-talk works great too.

Keeping poise is yet another great self-esteem booster. Losing your nerve, yelling, taking revenge, etc., all these things can really take a serious toll on your self-image, because that is the *weak and easy response*. On the other hand, having a calm and respectful demeanor with difficult people, forgiving what is hard to forgive, and handling difficult situations in a non-reactive way, is not only **hugely** beneficial to build better relationships and a great life, but also, it is a strong and noble character trait that, when you develop, will surely improve how you feel about yourself.

Set your boundaries, my friend! If someone addresses you in a disrespectful manner, calmly and respectfully tell them that you do not accept that kind of treatment. Create healthy boundaries of space, belongings, attitude, etc. Likewise, respect the boundaries of others. Like Lisa Nichols wisely said: "The world is looking at you and following your example on how to treat you."

Lastly, confront REALITY. How are your finances? How's your health? How about career and love life? When our self-esteem is a bit hurt, *denial* is a natural tendency, for we feel the need to protect ourselves and create the illusion that everything is okay. The fact is, by being in denial, all that will get progressively worse. Successful people work with the facts, admit their mistakes and *take responsibility*, fixing things as quickly as possible in order to not repeat the same errors again. What can you DO about what's not right in your life?

Start there and start NOW. Set your goals (chapter 08), take action (chapter 10), profit from failure (chapter 11), and even reinvent yourself (chapter 25) if you have to!

In sum, self-esteem is a form of internal success, an emotional immune system, and the reputation that you acquire with yourself. To have good basic self-esteem you must *live in integrity*, and you improve it even further by *doing hard things*. A healthy self-esteem leads to better relationships, finances, health and is the basis of a happier life.

JUMPSTART

Chapter 7

4.5 pages | 5 minutes

Beliefs

Give all the money and the most favorable circumstances to a person with the wrong beliefs, and that person will be sure to fail. Give the heaviest adversities to a person with the right beliefs and that person will most likely succeed.

- Beliefs are to the mind as railroads are to a train.
- The *master key* for a successful and happy life is a healthy set of beliefs.
- Beliefs can be created and destroyed by managing your FAITH investment in it.
- Genuinely *growing up* is releasing other people's belief systems and creating your own.

Belief is basically a THOUGHT in which you have invested a lot of FAITH. Not religious faith, but the kind of faith that you're certain about something—just like you have faith that tomorrow the sun will rise, and you will wake up to live another day. It's a solid certainty.

For example, the belief that *money is hard to get* may begin with the thought that *apparently* money doesn't come easy. By putting your attention and focus on everything that indicates and confirms that, as well as internalizing the perspective of the very people around you that struggle with money, you grow more and more faith in this thought until it becomes a *belief*. As a result, you become certain that a person must be very lucky to be rich, that this "rich thing" is not for you or for the average Joe. This *limiting belief* can become so strong that you won't even *dare* to do something with potential for great monetary gain—it just *seems impossible*, so *why even bother trying*?

It may not be your fault that ou have limiting beliefs, but it is your responsibility to change them. As we were growing up, our brains were searching for beliefs to navigate life—it was required for survival and understanding *how the world works*. At the same time, we were too young to select these beliefs in our best interest. You couldn't say, "This is a limiting belief; I'll pass on this one." So, you just absorbed, like a sponge, the beliefs from the people closest to you, especially from your family and friends. If you grew up in a house with your parents fighting, chances are that you created the limiting belief that marriages can't be happy, and as a consequence, you may have trouble with your own marriage in the future. If you grew up in a low-income neighborhood, you may have created the limiting belief that money is scarce, and therefore, you will have trouble finding a highly profitable job or creating a successful business. That's why most people born in the ghetto stay in the ghetto—they tend to think and act within the confines of the common limiting beliefs of the people from their zip code. But there are those that make it out of the ghetto and step into success, like Oprah! The difference is that those who are successful have learned to see through the predominant belief system of where they came from and believed in something better. In other words, they escaped *the matrix*.

If you are still living by the beliefs that you *borrowed* from others, then you're simply not living YOUR life! You're living what life is *supposed* to be from the viewpoint of those from whom you inherited the beliefs. It can't be your life if you're not the author of it. When you were young, you didn't have a choice, but now you do. What would your life look like WITHOUT these inherited limiting beliefs? What would your life be like guided by the beliefs that YOU strategically and consciously choose to live by? Now is the time to say, "Guys, thanks for letting me borrow your beliefs, they got me by. Now excuse me, I'm going to take the driver's seat and come up with beliefs of my own."

JUMPSTART

The day that you reinvent your belief system based upon your OWN judgement, you become your-SELF. That's what I call *genuinely growing up*; it's not the age, not the job, not the marriage, not the bills to pay. Growing up is breaking free from the reality of others and creating your own. Wake up, take the *red pill* and go live YOUR life, once and for all!

Now you know that THOUGHT + FAITH = BELIEF. Therefore, by managing your *faith investments* you manage your beliefs. The spell of a limiting belief is broken when you withdraw your faith in it. To do so, you must play the *devil's advocate* in your mind by asking the questions and looking for evidence that debunks the limiting belief that you want to break—effectively proving yourself wrong about it. Once your faith is no longer there, you can reinvest this faith in a new empowering thought, thereby creating a new empowering belief in place. You do that with the reverse process, by advocating in favor of this new empowering thought and looking for evidence that supports it, thus turning it into a belief—proving yourself right about it.

Alternatively, you can also *modify* the very thought that is the foundation of a limiting belief, with the purpose of transforming it into an empowering belief. The faith is there already, so you don't need to *reinvest* your faith. For example, I had the belief that I was so broken emotionally that I would never be a normal person. The original thought is that *I've been broken <u>beyond repair</u>*. One day, I asked myself the question, "What happens when a bone breaks?" Well, the answer is, *it heals stronger*. Therefore, to change that original limiting belief, I've replaced the *'beyond repair'* with *'it heals stronger.'* It was a pretty simple change, but it transformed me. I feel that because I've been broken and healed so many times, I have what it takes to stand tall when times are rough, more than most people, and I am thankful for that. That's how you change a limiting belief into an empowering one. Make an inventory of your limiting beliefs and decide which ones you will change into an empowering belief, and which ones you will debunk to create new, empowering beliefs in their place.

There's one sneaky belief that we pretty much ALL have and it is a major impediment for our progress and freedom. It's the belief that "I have to be right." First, it is a major roadblock for all kinds of relationships. Second, we don't learn anything by being *right in our opinion*. Instead, we learn when we are wrong and find out what is *right in reality*. Third, to change your limiting beliefs you need to prove yourself wrong about them. Examples: "It's impossible to make money doing what you love," "I am not good enough to be successful," or "I am not healthy and never will be." WHY would you ever want to be right about things like that?! Being WRONG about it is much, much better. Think long and hard about things in which you believe you're right, but about which you're better off being wrong. Then look for the evidence that proves you are wrong.

Beliefs can be divided into two categories: the ones that OPEN the possibility of success, and the ones that CLOSE it. The following tale demonstrates that clearly:

A long time ago, two shoe salesmen were sent to Africa. They both called back to the office. The first salesman reported: "No one here wears any shoes, there is no market for us here!" The second salesman reported: "No one here wears any shoes, there is a huge market for us, send inventory fast!"

Which one has a chance of succeeding in doing business in Africa? The second, of course! His optimism may be a little out of hand, but at least he has the chance, because he is *willing to try* and put in the work required. The first salesman has no chance whatsoever, because of his limiting belief, he won't even try to do business there. What the second salesman needs is a dose of healthy skepticism, in this case, doing the math: verifying the spending power of the population, checking how much it costs to import the shoes, what the fixed costs are, etc. If the numbers check out OK, now he can use his optimism to fuel his hope and enthusiasm, which CERTAINLY will help propel his business forward!

Imagine that you just closed a deal on a car. You can drive it home believing you made a super deal, or believing you bought a P.O.S. car

JUMPSTART

that will break very soon. Same car, same facts, but one belief makes you *feel good*, and the other belief makes you *feel bad*. Which belief is best? NEITHER. Why? Because in reality the car is decent, the deal was not bad but wasn't amazing. Both beliefs are *inaccurate,* therefore, you should not believe either of them. Too many people get trapped in *feeling good* about their ideas and beliefs. Always assume the position of a skeptic and GIVE YOURSELF a reality check before others do. This is especially true for businesses and relationships—always check the facts. The formula is simple:

1- Start with the beliefs that OPEN the possibilities for success.
2- Have a healthy dose of skepticism.
3- Ask HOW to succeed.
4- WORK on it.

Chapter 8

5 pages | 7 minutes

Setting Worthwhile Goals

"There is no passion to be found playing small, in settling for a life that is less than the one you are capable of living."—Nelson Mandela.

- In success or defeat, worthy goals are always better for you.
- Mediocre goals shrink your horizons, hurt your confidence and self-esteem.
- Long-term goals do not require you to know exactly how you're going to achieve them.
- Short-term goals need to be specific, practical and actionable steps.
- Don't overestimate what you can do in one year, and don't underestimate what you can do in five years.

Incredibly enough, many people fail to accomplish their goals, not because they've set them too high, but because they've set them too low. For this very reason, they aren't *driven* enough to accomplish it. In other words, if you can't get excited about your goals, then you're doing it wrong. You want to set them *high enough and then some*. The risk of failure (chapter 11) always exists, even for small and petty goals. So, why risk failing at something mediocre?

By working towards an audaciously worthy goal, you *do* your best and you *become* your best. Even if you find temporary defeat, you can look back and appreciate how far you've come just by giving that big and worthy goal a shot. The appreciation and acknowledgement that you've learned a great deal, is where you will find the faith and the strength to not give up and continue the mission—and eventually succeed.

In reality, failure and progress are mutually exclusive. If you gained something from pursuing your goal, you've succeeded, even if you haven't obtained (entirely or in part) the goal that you envisioned just yet. If your goal is truly worthy, you won't just "leave it at that," but instead, you'll pick yourself up and keep doing what it takes, finding alternatives, working around problems, muscling through whatever you need, until you succeed. You become UNSTOPPABLE! (chapter 16)

If that didn't convince you to set audaciously worthy goals, this might just do the trick: do you know what happens if you fail to accomplish a mediocre goal? It MESSES YOU UP. That's the *loser's dilemma*, they fail to accomplish what they *don't even want* in the first place, and as a result, aim each time lower in a downward spiral. It takes a toll on your confidence, and even on your self-esteem (chapter 6). By avoiding mediocre goals, you're actually *protecting yourself* by eliminating the possibility of failing at something petty. "Go big or go home," my friend. I know this sounds a bit ridiculous, but there is much truth to that. Maybe the sales engineers from Apple would've failed at selling lemonade on the street, you'll never know!

How about you and I make a pact? *We're NOT going to allow ourselves to risk failing at anything that we don't care about or don't even want, and we WILL go all out in taking our very best shot at everything that we care about and long for.* DEAL?! (Hi-Five goes here).

Your goals are best divided in two categories, Long-term (LT) and Short-term (ST). Set your ST goals to keep you taking action (chapter 10) and building momentum, and your LT goals as milestones to attain what you call a successful life. With clearly defined goals, you can best direct your time, money and efforts to jumpstart building the life that YOU want.

Your ST goals need to be actionable steps towards your LT goals, with clearly defined key results. This may sound silly, but along with your goals, you need to define a metric by which you'll measure the results for you to know that you're on the right track. For example, if one of your LT goals is to get to an old age in good health, you can set different ST goals to jumpstart healthy habits (chapter 09) such as exercising and eating well. Measurable key results could be for example, your cholesterol markers, or not getting sick for a year as a result of an improved immune system—I'm actually celebrating this one, 18 months and counting!

As I mentioned earlier, setting lowball goals is a terrible practice. HOWEVER, there is nothing wrong in setting *humble* key results and building your way up—sometimes it will be necessary; it could be as humble as losing one pound of weight in a month, saving $1000 in a year, or taking less than five minutes to finish parallel parking (giggles)—as long as it represents measurable progress!

No matter how bad the situation is regarding what you want to improve, whether that is health, finances, or even your love life, you should NOT aim for any less than unquestionably worthwhile for your LT goals. In cases like this, where you're starting from a seemingly bad place, it will be necessary to set realistic and attainable key results that are sized appropriately for you to have that inspiring *win*, one after another, which may be small at first, but progressively bolder and greater over time—what matters most is to *get moving*.

In sum, set your LT goals to be worthy and exciting—you must feel successful once you achieve them! Set your ST goals as milestones to accomplish your LT goals. Create expectations for key results that are realistic and compatible with each phase of your life. To better illustrate the use of LT and ST goals and their respective key results, please find as a bonus to this chapter the history of Ray: A 25-year-old gentleman that graduated with 23k in student loan debt, who managed to pay off his debt in just two years and become a millionaire before the age of 40. Disclosure: it's not a real-life history, but it's definitely down to earth and attainable by most people.

The moment that you set your goals, immediately, you will start seeing opportunities where you didn't see any before. New ideas will

JUMPSTART

begin to bubble up. These ideas and opportunities will be the bridge from where you *are* now, to where you *are* happier and more accomplished in the future. It's no accident that I used "you are" for both "now" and "in the future."

Think of life as a timeline in which the beginning represents when you are born, and the end represents when you are gone; right now you are at a point somewhere between the beginning and the end, and so are your LT goals—just a bit more offset to the right from where you are; your LT goals *are there* on this timeline, therefore, they exist. Like Denzel Washington said, "It's yours already, you just have to claim it." You claim it by honoring the ideas that will come to you for the realization of your LT goals and taking action upon them.

If you have difficulty intentionally setting a firm age by which to accomplish an LT goal, I recommend that you literally draw up this timeline and, by letting your hand do the work, you set that due date *by feeling*. With a 12-inch / 30-centimeter ruler, draw a 30 cm line. This is a 3:1 scale of the timeline of your life; zero represents birth, and 30 represents 90 years of age. Now, mark a point corresponding exactly to your age; for example, if you're 25, you divide 25 by 3 and at 8.3 centimeters you mark a dot—that's where you are at. If you're 56, divide 56 by 3 and at 18.6 centimeters, you mark a dot. Now, think of a specific LT goal, look at your timeline and just let your hand mark the new dot in the future, wherever it feels reasonable. Now you can measure how far this new dot is from zero, multiply by three, and discover the age by which you unconsciously deem it possible to achieve your LT goal. For example, if you are currently 25 and if you marked a dot representing "financial success" at 11.5 cm, that would represent the age of 34 and a half.

The magic about LT goals is that, at the very time that you set them, *you don't need to know how to get there*. For example, you could set an LT goal to get married in five years. You don't know how it's going to happen and you cannot control it very much, but the moment you set your mind to it, your focus and efforts will be unconsciously directed in a way that this might just happen in about five years (give or take). Never underestimate the power of your subconscious mind, my friend! It works as a *magnet*.

Unlike your LT goals, your ST goals need to be practical and actionable steps within your reach today. The more specific and detailed you are about them, the better. The majority of your ST goals should be set anywhere between a day and up to one year—usually. You want a clear mission that you can see through, and a clear time frame for it.

One non-negotiable about ST goals is that it *must* require more dedication and effort than your average in order to develop your discipline and your ability to grow. Make it a game to do more than you initially planned for, challenging yourself to surpass your own expectations. For example, if you set an ST goal to read a book in six months, read it in just three or four—this will make you gain a positive *reputation with yourself*. The more you surpass the mark, the more you're creating the habit of PLAYING TO WIN. The whole purpose of ST goals is to completely curb any margin of "I'm trying," "I'm working on it," or the "I will get around to that eventually" type of BS. When it comes to your life, remember that you are your own boss—make yourself proud of *you*!

If you say, "Oh, but I don't have a goal," well, that is just NOT true. Your most obvious ST goal is to make the best of TODAY (chapter 27), and your most obvious LT goal is to become who you've always wanted to be. If "who you've always wanted to be" is not yet clear to you, simply make a list of the five people you admire the most and why you admire them. Single out their character traits that you value the most, as well as the great things in life that they've accomplished and that you would like to conquer for yourself. Piece it all together, and there you have it: the perfect mosaic of who you want to become—which is your ultimate LT goal. Now you have your starting point and your ending point—no excuses, my friend. Go ahead, grab a pen and a paper and start writing down your ST goals and LT goals. Don't forget to sign and date it!

JUMPSTART

The History of Ray

9 pages | 12 minutes

From Student Loan to Financial Freedom

This is the hypothetical history of Ray, which is inspired by the reality of many people in their 20s. In real life there will be other expenses unaccounted for, such as a car breaking down, buying furniture, paying medical bills, unexpected issues, etc. But if you organize your finances well, even with these setbacks you can still pay your debt, save a good sum of money, and invest in your future. Please read Chapter 21 for information about how to optimally manage your money.

Imagine that Ray is 25, freshly graduated with a student loan debt of **$23k**. Ray's start is not the best; like many, not only does he not have a job yet, but he has no savings, drives an old car, and needs to pay off his student loan. However, none of that is a problem for Ray, because he is going to set his goals and work through them. Ray has two LT goals:

The first is to be living comfortably, with no debt, plus having at least one year's worth of savings by the age of 30. He knows: you're doing yourself a favor by saving up money even before you figure out what's next, because when that time comes, more options will be available for you.

The second LT goal is to be financially free before the age of 40, so he no longer needs to trade his invaluable time (chapter 02) for money by working a full-time job to pay the bills—a truly worthy LT goal!

The first short-term (ST) goal that Ray has set is to pay off his debt in just two years, by the age of 27. To do so, Ray did the math and verified that he needs to put **$970** dollars every month towards paying off his student loan for the next two years. However, Ray's first job paid him just 34k/year, or **$1,983** per month after tax. Because his first job wasn't so great, Ray talked with his parents about his goals, and asked to move in with them just *until* he finds a higher paying job. For the first year, every month Ray has set aside **$200** in a savings account, which is about 10% of his income, paid **$970** of the loan, and used the remaining **$813** for his expenses—such as gym membership, groceries, and paying half of the utilities bill for his parents, beer with friends, etc.

Salary	**$1,983.00**
Student Loan Payment	**$970.00**
Savings for the future	**$200.00**
All other expenses (below)	**$813.00**
Rent	$0.00
Utilities (helping parents)	$100.00
Groceries	$250.00
Car Insurance	$60.02
Gym	$30.00
Spotify	$9.99
Amazon Prime	$12.99
Gas	$70.00
Fun money	$280.00

Ray's <u>first</u> year of employment, making 34k.

		January	February	March	April	May	June
		1	2	3	4	5	6
Year 1	Savings	$200	$400	$600	$800	$1,000	$1,200
	Debt - Student Loan	-$22,030	-$21,060	-$20,090	-$19,120	-$18,150	-$17,180
		July	August	September	October	November	December
		7	8	9	10	11	12
	Savings	$1,400	$1,600	$1,800	$2,000	$2,200	**$2,400**
	Debt - Student Loan	-$16,210	-$15,240	-$14,270	-$13,300	-$12,330	-$11,360

Monthly progress on paying the debt and building savings.

JUMPSTART

Ray's first year key results were: debt reduced from 23k to **$11,360**, plus **$2,400** in savings—pretty good!

During that first year working a rather low paying job, Ray didn't waste time and built his LinkedIn presence; to do that, Ray looked for tips on YouTube on how to create a strong LinkedIn profile. As a result, Ray managed to switch over to a much better job, paying him $62k/year, or **$3,617** per month after tax. As a result, Ray rented a one bedroom apartment for himself and moved out of his parents' place. Every month Ray has set aside **$400** in a savings account, paid **$970** of the loan, and used the remaining **$2,247** for his expenses, including **$1,100** in rent—quite an upgrade in lifestyle!

- Groceries: $250 → $350
- Fun Money: $280 → $430
- Gas: $70 → $90

Salary	$3,617.00
Student Loan Payment	$970.00
Savings for my future	$400.00
All other expenses (below)	$2,247.00
Rent	$1,100.00
Utilities	$164.00
Groceries	$350.00
Car Insurance	$60.02
Gym	$30.00
Spotify	$9.99
Amazon Prime	$12.99
Gas	$90.00
Fun money	$430.00

Ray's <u>second</u> year of employment, making 62k.

		January	February	March	April	May	June
Year 2		1	2	3	4	5	6
	Savings	$2,800	$3,200	$3,600	$4,000	$4,400	$4,800
	Debt - Student Loan	-$10,390	-$9,420	-$8,450	-$7,480	-$6,510	-$5,540
		July	August	September	October	November	December
		7	8	9	10	11	12
	Savings	$5,200	$5,600	$6,000	$6,400	$6,800	$7,200
	Debt - Student Loan	-$4,570	-$3,600	-$2,630	-$1,660	-$690	PAID

Monthly progress on paying the debt and building savings.

Ray's second year key results were: NO DEBT and **$7,200** in savings. Not only did Ray meet his goal of paying off the student loan in just two years, but he surpassed the mark by having an additional 7.2k in savings—say "bye bye" to debt and "hello" to security! ST goal #1 SMASHED.

Now, as a debt-free 27 year old with a decent but not stellar job, Ray focused on his first LT goal, which is to have one year's worth of living expenses saved up—Ray knows that having these savings will give him good freedom to operate, switch jobs if he has to, invest when opportunity arises, etc. At work, everyone noticed that something is different about Ray, as he seems more driven, energetic, and committed. While his coworkers would slowly walk to grab a coffee and chat about the weather, Ray seemed to not waste any time. The truth is that none of his colleagues had clearly defined goals, but he did; Ray had a sense of urgency, purpose and a clear direction.

In order to fulfill his first LT goal, Ray has set the second ST goal of "maxing out" his salary at his current job, and therefore, saving more money every month. As Ray really got the hang of his work by the second year and began exceeding expectations, he asked for a raise (chapter 20). His superiors happily granted him a significant bump from 62k to 75k/year. Consequently, his monthly take-home pay was a better **$4,375.00**, starting from his third year working there. Relieved from paying the student loan, Ray decided to set aside a whopping **$1200** per month, instead of the previous **$400**. That would grow his savings much, much faster. Also, because Ray decided

JUMPSTART

to treat himself to a nicer vehicle, which he more than deserves at that point. There's nothing wrong with a healthy form of gratification (chapter 15). He purchased a really nice, low mileage used car for 12k, which he fully financed; his new car payment was **$352** for 36 months. Ray also upgraded his budget for lifestyle and moved into a bigger 2-bedroom apartment.

- Groceries: $350 → $400
- Fun Money: $430 → $700
- Rent: $1,100 → $1,300
- Gas: $90 → $125

Salary	$4,375.00
Car Payment	$352.00
Savings for my future	$1,200.00
All other expenses (below)	$2,823.00
Rent	$1,300.00
Utilities	$172.00
Groceries	$400.00
Car Insurance	$73.02
Gym	$30.00
Spotify	$9.99
Amazon Prime	$12.99
Gas	$125.00
Fun money	$700.00

Ray's <u>third to fifth</u> year of employment, making 62k.

Year 3		January	Feburary	March	April	May	June
		1	2	3	4	5	6
	Savings	$8,400	$9,600	$10,800	$12,000	$13,200	$14,400
	Debt - Car Payment	-$12,306	-$11,954	-$11,602	-$11,250	-$10,898	-$10,546
		July	August	September	October	November	December
		7	8	9	10	11	12
	Savings	$15,600	$16,800	$18,000	$19,200	$20,400	**$21,600**
	Debt - Student Loan	-$10,194	-$9,842	-$9,490	-$9,138	-$8,786	**-$8,434**

Year 4		January	Feburary	March	April	May	June
		1	2	3	4	5	6
	Savings	$22,800	$24,000	$25,200	$26,400	$27,600	$28,800
	Debt - Car Payment	-$8,082	-$7,730	-$7,378	-$7,026	-$6,674	-$6,322
		July	August	September	October	November	December
		7	8	9	10	11	12
	Savings	$30,000	$31,200	$32,400	$33,600	$34,800	**$36,000**
	Debt - Student Loan	-$5,970	-$5,618	-$5,266	-$4,914	-$4,562	**-$4,210**

Year 5		January	Feburary	March	April	May	June
		1	2	3	4	5	6
	Savings	$37,200	$38,400	$39,600	$40,800	$42,000	$43,200
	Debt - Car Payment	-$3,858	-$3,506	-$3,154	-$2,802	-$2,450	-$2,098
		July	August	September	October	November	December
		7	8	9	10	11	12
	Savings	$44,400	$45,600	$46,800	$48,000	$49,200	**$50,400**
	Debt - Student Loan	-$1,746	-$1,394	-$1,042	-$690	-$338	**PAID**

Monthly progress on paying the debt and building savings.

After three years living very comfortably like this, his key results for his 30th birthday were: NO DEBT, a good car fully paid for, and a whopping **$50,400** in savings—cash. ST goal #2 SMASHED!

As a 30 year old man with over 50k in savings, Ray began to research different ways in which he could invest his savings to further build his wealth. The truth is that, although he was getting to save **$14,400** per year with his job, that wasn't enough to take him to financial freedom. Let's pause here for a second and cherish the fact that, at this point, Ray had successfully gotten his life together. Now he is just figuring out how to *expand* his life to what he calls success. Everything from here on out, no longer has the pressure and the burden of scarcity, debt, and living with parents. He's already free from that stuff! Every gain from here on, is focused on his happiness and goals, instead of the basics.

JUMPSTART

In order to make his LT goal of financial freedom come true, Ray would need to figure out *something else*—read Disrupt your approach, Chapter 25. Ray had no particular passion, but he was somewhat handy and a really hard-worker, and for this reason, Ray decided to take his chances with Real Estate (RE). Another year working at his regular job passed by while Ray kept up his savings rate, and at the same, researching how to get started with RE. As expected, when Ray's 31st birthday came along, his key results were: No debt, and **$64,800** in savings.

$$\$50,400 + (12 \text{ months} \times \$1,200) = \$64,800.00$$

To jumpstart his RE journey, Ray set the third ST goal of purchasing a "fixer upper" house, renovating and selling it for a profit in order to get to his 32nd birthday knowing how to flip homes—a very usable skill. Although his 65k in savings most likely wasn't enough, Ray started discussing his ideas of investing in RE with his coworker friend Bob, who seemed to be highly interested. Bob also had significant savings, and together, they decided to take action (chapter 10) and get down to business. Like Ray, Bob was also trustworthy and had a great work ethic (chapter 13).

After working through some serious whoopsies, doing quite a bit of the laborious work themselves, and learning invaluable lessons for their next deals, both Ray and Bob netted a rather modest profit of just $6k each on their first house flip. That's quite an underwhelming profit. It just didn't go as well as they hoped; they hired people that didn't deliver and the house had more repairs to be done than they anticipated. However, not only did they manage to still make some money in spite of the unforeseen issues, but next time around they will *know better*. They will know who to hire and who not to hire, what suppliers have the best prices, how to best spend money to add value to a property. They've acquired *experience* and began building their *network*. In fact, they learned so much that even if they had no profit whatsoever, it would still be great gain, because failing and learning are mutually exclusive. Ray's 32nd birthday key results were: **$85,200** in savings and the newly acquired "flipping houses" skill. ST goal #3 SMASHED!

$64,800 + (12 months x $1,200) + $6,000 = $85,200.00

Although Ray's first RE deal was difficult and not very profitable, he didn't chicken-out. Sure enough, Ray and Bob started pumping up each other's enthusiasm again, looking for new and better RE investment opportunities. With a little more money at their disposal and some real-world experience, lo and behold, in one year they managed to flip, not one, but two properties, netting a much higher 27k each! As the gains got better and the process got easier, they began truly enjoying this side-hustle (chapter 18). Not only was Ray on his way to meet his LT goal of financial freedom, but he was actually having a good time while doing so. The truth is that it's much better to fall in love with the process, than with the result, because the process is guaranteed, the result is not!

Ray's 33rd birthday key results were: much improved "flipping houses" skill and **$126,600** in savings— that's 6 digits on his bank account! Even more important than that, is how much better he got at this new and profitable skill.

$85,200 + (12 months x $1,200) + $27,000 = $126,600.00

Ray and Bob were getting more excited about it each time. Not only did their side-hustle become very profitable, but it became easier and more enjoyable. Ray and Bob kept flipping properties and automating the whole process with self-motivated contractors, to the point that they became comfortable flipping up to four properties a year—while still working their full-time jobs! At that point, they did the math and came to the easy conclusion that it would be a greater gain to quit their jobs and work full time with Real Estate, further expanding and accelerating their operation.

JUMPSTART

At the age of 40, Ray had over two million dollars of equity in several cash flowing properties, collecting enough rent to afford a comfortable life without having to work at all. LT goal #2, SMASHED! Ray kept working at his convenience, out of joy and the desire to keep growing, and he began mentoring others like him to get out of the slavery of debt and into a comfortable life.

<u>The Bottom Line</u>: Ray started off with 23k in debt and no job. Once he got his first job, he made just 34k in his first year. From there, he got a second and better job, which he made 62k between his second and third year, and 75k from his third year and onwards—until he no longer needed the full-time job, of course.

Nothing out of the ordinary, nothing stellar. He didn't work for Google or Microsoft, nor was he a genius of any kind or extraordinarily talented. Yet, because he set his goals correctly, delayed gratification enough, and had a strong work ethic, he came out on top. In fact, Ray got much farther ahead than most of his colleagues from school that he considered brilliant and talented.

Chapter 9

4 pages | 5 minutes

Your Habits

The quality of your life is mostly determined by the quality of your habits. Knowledge, ambitions, talents, goals, etc. are all great, but at the end of the day, what matters is what you are DOING on a daily basis to move towards those goals. Replacing counterproductive habits for constructive ones is a non-negotiable requirement for mastering your finances, health, happiness, and consequently, success.

- Your habits must support your goals.
- It only takes between 21 to 66 days to make or break a habit.
- Habits and self-esteem are intrinsically connected.
- Constructive habits bring joy and happiness.
- The formation of one good habit triggers the formation of other good habits, just like breaking one bad habit motivates you to break more bad habits.

Generally, people overestimate what they can do short term and underestimate what they can do long term. New Year's resolutions are a good example. Many people vow, "I'm going to meet these six goals this year!" but then find that not even half of their resolutions are met by the next New Year. However, people completely underestimate what they can do long-term through the formation of good habits. You can positively transform your finances, health, social circle and overall circumstances in just a few years by creating habits that support your long-term goals.

JUMPSTART

You can't expect everything to happen in one year or less. In two years, I eliminated signs of pre-diabetes, solved my GERD problem, and got in excellent athletic shape by creating the habits of waking up early, preparing my own meals, and exercising. In three years, I went from having just $200 in the bank and no credit (as a new U.S. resident) to having an entire year's worth of savings and an excellent credit score by creating the habits of over-delivering at work and saving 30% of my modest income. After these excellent results, I added another great habit to the pile: creating value (Chapter 23) for a minimum of three hours a day. This book is the result of that additional habit.

<u>Specific goals can't always be met, but habits can always be formed</u>. If you say, "I'm going to lose 50 pounds," you may lose 40 but never get to 50. Now, if you say, "I'm going to eat healthy and exercise four times a week," that is completely under your control—it's a failsafe strategy. The key is to accept that good things often take time to happen and that creating good habits are the seeds of a life worth living. Shoot for the long-term, and the results of your habits will flourish, often sooner than you think.

Habits, good or bad, all become automatic. Once a habit is formed, it no longer requires much of an effort; you just do it on *autopilot*. By bringing awareness to your habits, in place of destructive habits that lead to debt and failure, you create habits that lead to success and fulfillment. Breaking or creating habits does require effort, but not for long: usually 21 days for the little stuff and 66 days for the bigger stuff.

The spark of your enthusiasm just needs to last long enough to ignite the firewood of the habit that will keep burning indefinitely. For anxious people like me, even 21 days sounds like a lot, but really, it represents only 0.06% of one year out of the many years you still have to live. Not bad! What is that compared to a lifetime of rewards—financial stability, good health, and good relationships?

While the firewood of the good habits keeps on burning, you're *progressing*. Just having nice things isn't the key to happiness, but progress is. Like Tony Robbins said, "You can have everything. The moment you stop progressing you start dying." Sure, it will take time to collect the material rewards of your newly created productive habits. But, as soon as you form them, you *immediately* become full of hope and perspective! Creating good habits not only helps you obtain what you want, but also makes you feel better during the process—enjoying the journey.

<u>You become your habits</u>. You are more successful when you love yourself, admire yourself, and build an amazing reputation with yourself. We've covered that in the Self-Esteem chapter 06. We want to stay consistent with our self-image, and that is how habits are formed—good or bad. If you have the habit of running, you see yourself as a runner. If you have the habit of smoking, you see yourself as a smoker. Consequently, what do the habits of overspending, procrastinating, lying, etc., make you? Ouch! By living purposefully, you can deliberately choose to tear down the habits that hurt your self-image and, in place, create the habits that build it. As a consequence, you actually become the best version of yourself! Without a doubt, you will never EVER regret becoming the best version of yourself—how could you? However, you can definitively regret not changing your destructive habits.

It is essential that you break the habits that deep inside make you feel unworthy of success, and in their place, create the habits that make you feel deserving of it. That applies to every area of your life, from finances to romance. For example, when you save and manage your money properly, when you do a good deal of charity donations, certainly you will feel more deserving of being wealthy. Watching a bunch of porn will probably get in the way of how deserving you feel of having a successful loving marriage, as well as your hopes of it ever happening.

What habits are draining your bank account? You need to know how much your habits cost. Put on a spreadsheet the cost of superfluous habits such as going out for drinks multiple times a week, shopping for unnecessary things, or always upgrading to the latest phone. You may be staggered with the amount you could instead save or invest in your health and career. It blows my mind that online training programs, such as those from uDemy, cost less than a vodka drink at the bar. For instance, I paid $9.99 for "The Complete Android Developer Course." It literally costs 10 bucks to learn how to create apps for smartphones, which you can sell to millions of people—that's insane! To be successful, you need to have your priorities straight, especially if money is short at the moment. If it comes down to another drink or an online training program, remind yourself of your commitment to make the better choices for the long-term. Long-term my friend, long-term!

More in particular, the habit of saving money conserves your earnings systematically, while building in you the confidence to make even more. It's hard to think creatively and go about your future with ingenuity and curiosity when money seems to be always lacking. Saving money sends a message to your mind that "there is enough and a little more," which helps to get you out of a survival mindset and into a creative one where you see opportunities and take calculated risks to fulfil your dreams. This alone is a good enough reason to create the habit of saving—and whether you save a little or a lot, the effect is the same.

The following habits are incredibly powerful to increase your odds of being successful:

1) The habit of creating value (chapter 23);
2) The habit of saving money;
3) The habit of investing in your future;
4) The habit of prioritizing and getting done first what matters most;
5) The habit of always finishing what you started;
6) The habit of delaying gratification (chapter 15).

Last but not least, when you successfully acquire one new good habit, you become naturally more inclined both to quit bad habits and form more new good habits. Habits have a compounding effect! If you create the habit of exercising regularly, surely, you'll be inclined to eat more healthily and perhaps reduce or quit drinking. Likewise, creating the habit of saving money makes you want to do something else to generate even more money. Simply choose one good habit to start with, consolidate it, and everything else will happen naturally. Soon you'll be compounding the financial, physical, and psychological benefits on your way to success. Can't beat that!

Chapter 10

5 pages | 7 minutes

Taking ACTION

George S. Patton said, "A good plan violently executed now is better than a perfect plan next week." I would add "because next week you can try another plan in case your current one fails."

- A job well done is better than a "perfect" job that never gets finished.
- Speed of implementation is key to success.
- Learning has zero value, unless combined with action.
- Start on impulse, work with patience and finish with excellence.

A fictional story:

As a kid, little Alissa used to be the most beautiful and joyful girl with her captivating smile and a shirt with paint stains. Her parents worked very hard and money was short, but that wasn't a problem for Alissa; all she needed was love, shelter, paint, and a brush—all of which she had.

By her mid 20's, you simply would not recognize Alissa anymore. Her face was tired, her excitement disappeared, and even her unique smile was gone. Her life was a grind. She was going to Law School because her parents insisted on it and she was babysitting, driving for Uber, and delivering food in order to make ends meet. Needless to say, she wasn't happy.

In the peak of her crisis, Alissa did what many people do: she went to a bar to medicate herself with alcohol. She asked the bartender for a vodka drink, as well as a pen, as she felt the desire to doodle on a napkin. She was hoping to get blindly drunk, but a funny thing happened. She was getting more joy and relief from drawing something again after all these years, than by drinking. Just before finishing her drawing of a rose on that napkin, Alissa got frustrated and threw it away. To her surprise, the bartender promptly rescued it from the trash, claiming that it was really beautiful, and he wanted to keep it.

    The next day, Alissa couldn't help but to think of how good it felt to draw again and get compliments from a complete stranger—she was excited! Both this excitement and the frustration of how *grey* her life had become, prompted her to doodle every morning and simply give these doodles away to the customers that she tended to in her side jobs. Sure enough, they started to show her lots of love and great tips! Even with the heavy workload, her days had not only become more bearable, but emotionally rewarding too.

    Encouraged by her customers and friends, Alissa decided to go back to painting like she did when she was little. Hesitantly, Alissa put a bit of money towards buying a few canvases, paints and a set of brushes. She figured that, just for how well it made her feel to do her craft, it would be worth it anyway. Alissa then began to sell her art online, which turned out to be increasingly profitable over time, in fact, much more than she ever imagined possible.

--

    Let's talk about the value of learning, which is zero. What is valuable is what you DO with what you have learned. Instead of trying to "know everything" so you can "do anything," inverse the whole process. First, define what it is that you need to do. Second, define what it is that you need to learn in order to accomplish that (if you can't hire it out). Third, learn only what is needed, leaving out all the unnecessary information, and put it to use. Without help, I've created products that would require at least two or three engineers for electronic, software and mechanical design. I believe that the key for those successes wasn't knowing everything, but instead, *not knowing* anything *useless*! Unless you're going to use it, don't learn it. You only have so much time, so, save it for what is useful and always <u>consolidate learning with execution</u>!

In itself, action is more valuable than learning because you can always learn from doing things, but you can never do anything by just learning. Alissa learned to paint simply by paint-*ing*. Reading a book is not taking action. Going to a seminar is not taking action. However, when you combine both <u>study and action</u> to accomplish something <u>clearly defined</u>, your rate of progress will be extraordinary, my friend. The power of learning resides in sparing you the time and failures from trying to do things without prior knowledge—as long as you always combine your learning with execution and spend no more time on *learning-only* than actually *doing things*. Summing up, learning alone has no value, action alone has limited value, action and learning combined is extremely valuable!

The speed of learning and execution is also key. We're all tired of knowing that Thomas Edison failed 1000 times before he could finally create the light bulb. What people don't get from this history is that, if he had taken a couple of months between each attempt, it would have taken him more than 150 working years to make it. The only reason he made it during his lifetime is that Edison failed FAST. The path is never straight. Whatever it is that you want to accomplish, you're going to have to try and fail until something sticks. Therefore, how fast you try things will determine how many things you get to try in your life, such as different businesses, products, services, or even jobs.

A job well-**done** is better than a perfect job. Whereas the perfect plan or job is either never finished or takes much longer to be completed, a job well-done is a measurable task completed. If you find yourself stuck and unable to finish what you started because it's not "perfect" yet, chances are that you need to develop a better relationship with criticism (chapter 12). If whatever you're trying to do fails, most likely it didn't fail because it wasn't perfect, but because it wasn't the right thing to do in the first place. IF what you're doing is right, especially in business, chances are that you will still succeed in spite of some errors. Within a reasonable timeframe, do your best work, always keeping in mind that the <u>law of diminishing returns</u> also applies to the time and effort you spend. For example, if I can create a good product in one year, spending yet another year perfecting it probably won't make it twice as good, but only marginally better—now I've lost one year that I could be selling it and getting actual valuable feedback from customers to further improve it. Therefore, spend enough time and effort to do something truly well done, and then stop there—that is where you draw the line between encouraging excellence and paralyzing perfectionism!

START ON AN IMPULSE! We can be motivated by many things, some good, others not so much. Alissa was both excited about creating art and getting recognition for her talent, as well as frustrated about how unfulfilling her life had become. Whether your motivator is positive or negative, it doesn't matter. What matters is that a motivator as such will prompt you to take action and that is how many businesses, services and products are created. Read about fundamentals of products and services on Chapter 24.

As an employee, every major accomplishment I had at Kicker was initiated on an impulse. I've even been granted the patent for one of these projects. This motivation, whether positive or negative, is like rocket fuel; it gets you all fired up! The only issue with rocket fuel is that if you're not careful, you may jump on things too fast, look for shortcuts, all of which have a tendency to fail and burn you. It's fine to start a project by impulse, as long as you execute it with patience and excellence—that's a winning strategy!

You do not need a perfect plan! Alissa "felt like painting" and she went for it, without a plan. Overplanning is the fastest way to stop you from taking action. This is called "analysis paralysis." When you plan ahead too much, you don't get excited, you get *fearful*. Your brain is very good at imagining every possible unhappy ending for whatever you want to try: switching jobs, starting your business, creating a

JUMPSTART

product, writing a book, starting a work-out plan, asking someone on a date, and the list goes on. Planning is good, but not in excess. Instead of planning every detail of the *path*, simply set your goals (Chapter 08) and do what you can do TODAY (Chapter 27) to accomplish them.

Even the smallest progress will feel joyful and rewarding. This is caused by the dopamine release in your brain. Drawing and painting didn't make Alissa's days harder, it made her days better, as with each piece done, each compliment received and each sale made, she got a hit of dopamine. This is how taking action encourages you to take even more action. Dopamine is the perfect stress modulator, because even when things get hard and the load is almost too much to bear, dopamine gets released by taking action and that will help you through the process. You know what else dopamine is? A powerful antidepressant. You don't get dopamine by planning. You get dopamine by DOING the things aligned with your goals. Get your *big dreams* out and break them down into small enough problems that you can solve on a regular basis. The joy of solving these problems will feed into your daily level of enthusiasm and optimism. Make a commitment to do the work at hand with excellence and the *path will unfold* for you—one day at a time, my friend!

Chapter 11

4.5 pages | 6 minutes

Leveraging Failure

Your life is a war. Your odds of winning this war—becoming successful—are directly proportional to your resilience and wisdom, obtained by fighting many battles and learning from them, respectively. Successful people fight and lose many battles, but they take the lessons learned, improve their process, and march forward right to the next one—they won't stop until they're victorious.

- Failing is a **process** that is required to improve your resilience, wisdom, and strategy.
- Failure is an **outcome**; it only exists if you choose to *stop the process* of fail-**ing**.
- Success is a **product** of the qualities acquired through the process of failing.

Imagine telling the history of your life without some major things going completely wrong. If you're "lucky," it would be something like the following: "I graduated from school, got a job, then got another job, didn't travel much, didn't take many risks, had a bunch of ideas and plans that I never tried, and then after 50 years in that box, I finally retired. Now I don't even know what to do with the time I have left." A person who lived the life that I just described was in the war but not fighting the war; being comfortable and not fulfilled at the same time is <u>failure to subject yourself TO failure</u>.

When you wholeheartedly engage in the battles that life brings to you, even with material loss, the mistakes that you will make will all add to your wisdom; your success is a product of the wisdom that you accrued. Wisdom doesn't come from avoiding failure; wisdom comes from working <u>through</u> failure. But not all failure is created equal:

Genuine failure is when we don't even fight the battles, or, when we fight the battles but won't learn the lessons from them. In both cases, <u>genuine failure is an outcome; it keeps us in failure</u>.

In the first case, we're living to avoid pain, or in other words, "not even trying." This is the most effective way to live a life that adds up to nothing in the end. Usually, that's the life of those who always take the safest path, even though their heart is trying to pull them in a completely different direction.

In the second case, we are halfway there, as we are engaging in the battles but failing to learn from them. Usually this includes blaming everyone and everything for our failures, in other words, "bitching." That's the worst deal; we already paid for the wisdom with the pain of the battle lost, but we're refusing to receive it. For example, there are a myriad of lessons to be learned from a failed relationship or business, but this wisdom will only make its way into your mind if you accept your mistakes and re-evaluate everything you've done. In this case, the next time around, you'll make sure you don't repeat those mistakes, thereby increasing your odds of success.

Perceived failure is when we fight and fail to win the battle but take away invaluable lessons with us. Perceived failure throws in our face everything that went wrong, including what WE can do better. It makes us uncomfortable and requires humility to face our own issues, but it rewards us with the greatest POWER of all—the power to change and progress. Even when perceived failure comes with a big loss, emotional or material, we will be able to see what the missing pieces of the puzzle are, and therefore, seek knowledge and help from people to fill in the gaps. <u>Perceived failure is a process; it pushes you forward</u>. It leads to success by incremental improvement. Put yourself out there—**F**ail, **L**earn, **I**mprove, and **R**epeat (FLIR). The faster you start the FLIR process, the quicker you will be victorious.

Imagine that there is a 5K route that you would like to run, but you're completely out of shape. You go there, and after running just 1K you feel like dying, your tongue is hanging out, and you're sweating like a waterfall. You can't help but to stop and go home. That is <u>not</u> failure, so long as you come back there the next day and run 1.1K. It doesn't matter how many times you need to go back there to run again; inevitably, you'll be progressing, and at some point, you will be able to complete the 5K! It is entirely your CHOICE to go back there to run time after time, or to throw in the towel, OR even worse, to never go there to begin with. The good thing about life is that <u>it is never "game over" until YOU say so</u>. You see, it is ultimately your DECISION to surrender to genuine failure, or to show up and do the FLIR process.

So far, I have been writing about giving your best and never quitting, correct? I'm sure you've heard this cliché before. Here is the twist: **I don't want to tell you to never quit a battle that is not right for you**. I want you to give your best and never quit the battles that ARE worthy of your blood, sweat, and tears; however, <u>there are cases in which quitting is not weak, but wise</u>. Allow me illustrate:

In my first year of high school, I was put in a classroom full of bullies. If I only so much as asked the teacher a question, the entire class would promptly "boo" me and throw a bunch of crumpled paper balls at me. I could have stayed there longer trying to make it work, trying to become friends with some of the students. Well, looking at what I was up against and the limited expectation of a positive outcome, I decided not to make the effort. Instead, I went down to the principal's office and just asked him to put me in a different classroom, or else I would transfer to a different school. It worked out great! My best friends today—18 years later—are from the classroom that I switched to. I couldn't be happier to have made that choice! Had I decided to stay in the first classroom and fight that battle, I wouldn't have the amazing friends I have today. The takeaway is that I didn't fail by not fighting that battle because it wasn't worth the fight to begin with. Quitting wasn't weak; it was wise!

JUMPSTART

Now, how does that apply in your life? What kind of battles are you fighting in your career and relationships? Before getting too excited about switching battles, honestly ask yourself the following:
1. Am I retiring from this battle to fight a BETTER battle?
2. Am I NOT running away from pain?
3. Have I unquestionably done my part for the process of FLIR to take place?

Be aware that, in a moment of weakness, you may be tempted to use this argument to *justify* quitting a battle that may very well be the right battle to fight. However, if you answered a solid YES to the three questions above, it's probably time to MOVE ON. Sometimes relationships, jobs, and businesses are either not worth fighting for or are too far gone to recover. That's when you need to *tactically retreat*, recover, then charge forward towards the next battle.

In our lives we must pick our battles; after all, we only have so much time (Chapter 02). Saying "yes" to one battle means saying "no" to other battles that are possibly better. Running yourself into the ground fighting a battle that is not worthwhile, when all the while you could be fighting a better battle, is <u>failure to choose wisely</u>. People glorify those that work hard, even when they're fighting a battle that makes no sense. What a waste! If you're trying to sell sand in the desert and you never give up when you could be selling coconuts on the beach instead, you're not determined and strong, you're just insisting on perpetuating the error—which is another form of genuine failure. Wars are won not only by brute force, but by strategy as well. We cover that in Chapter 25, about disrupting your approach.

The battles that are truly worth your blood, sweat, and tears are <u>aligned with your values</u>, with a potential outcome that is unquestionably worth the fight, no matter how hard it gets. More about becoming unstoppable in Chapter 16.

But what should you do if NONE of the battles in front of you seem to be worth the fight? Be strategic; pick the best out of the bunch! After all, you can only become a great warrior by PRACTICING. Therefore, if you don't know yet what the battle of your life is, be assured that by fighting seemingly unworthy battles (e.g., working a night shift at a low paying job), you are preparing yourself for the big one. You don't become a good warrior by being picky about your battles, sitting around waiting for the perfect battle that meets your requirements! You become a failure by doing that. If today's battle consists of selling sand in the desert, then SELL the freaking sand in the desert! That will make you a hell of a salesman. If tomorrow you get to sell coconuts on the beach, for damn sure you will outsell every other salesman that didn't have it as hard as you did. Just like paramedics practice CPR on a dummy, build yourself up by fighting the best battle that is at hand while actively going after better battles to fight. You want to be prepared for the REAL battle—and believe me, it will come.

Chapter 12

4 pages | 5 minutes

Dealing with Criticism

The more you stand out, the more criticism you will get. By handling it constructively, it will help you achieve your goals while creating an excellent reputation for yourself.

- Criticism is like a walnut in the shell; you can't swallow it whole!
- We need criticism to succeed because we can't get everything right the first time. It's the best feedback mechanism.
- To benefit from criticism, we need good self-esteem.
- Criticizing may build or undermine trust depending on the words you use.

Often, listening to criticism is the difference between progressing or being stuck in life. As an employee, it may be the difference between getting fired or promoted. In leadership (chapter 14), it may be the difference between being loved or hated by those you lead. As a spouse, it may be the difference between having a loving and stable marriage or divorce. As an entrepreneur, it can be the difference between being massively successful or entirely rejected by the market.

The key to benefiting from criticism is not to take it personally. That is easier said than done—especially when the criticism is directed at something that you created, or even worse, at you! It takes a good deal of self-esteem to take criticism well, but once the emotional charge is removed from it, all that is left, hopefully, is the much-needed feedback to help you, my friend!

No one should expect to "get everything right" the first time. For this reason, the error information contained within criticism helps us correct, optimize, and become successful in all spheres of life, starting with our own behavior and relationships and ending with the things that we create and do.

Think of criticism as a walnut in the shell. Swallowing it whole would cause some serious damage, but if you crack the shell and get to the core of it, it is good and healthy for you. Self-esteem (Chapter 06) is the tool that allows you to crack that shell open without hurting yourself and get to what matters.

There are three types of criticism:

1. **A Rotten Walnut:** Occurrence is rare. It has no value; it is purely generated from antagonism, jealousy, etc. Example: "You suck! You're really dumb and incompetent." This provides you with no useful information because it doesn't tell you *why* you are supposedly incompetent, dumb, etc. If your self-esteem is healthy, you're able to discard this kind of criticism altogether. Forgive and forget!

2. **A Shelled Walnut:** Occurrence is frequent. At its core, there is the invaluable information that you may need to be successful. It is, however, enclosed in the "hard shell" of frustration, anger, even cruelty towards you. Use your self-esteem tool to crack that shell and get to the nutritious core of it. Example: "Your online classes suck because you don't even have a Q&A section. Only an idiot would do that!" Despite the insult, this criticism contains the useful information that a Q&A section is missing. Implementing the Q&A section will improve the online classes and its odds of success. Good stuff!

3. **An Unshelled Walnut:** Occurrence depends on how much you allow people to be honest with you without "lashing out" at them. It's the type of criticism that comes from an honest friend. Listening carefully to this sort of criticism can spare you from a lot of pain and disappointment. It will point out your shortcomings, on which you can improve or get someone else's help. Someone else's help might even look like hiring or creating a partnership. For example, if someone criticizes your idea to open a business by saying, "I don't think you're

ready to have your own business yet. You get seriously overwhelmed when you have to deal with multiple tasks and freak out when things don't go as planned." If you see this as an unshelled walnut, you can partner with someone who has the ability to split tasks with you and make alternate plans on the fly. Problem solved!

At the end of 2017, I was finishing up the creation of the [Kicker Key Amplifier](). It was my first project at Kicker, the company that sponsored me to come to the U.S. I felt that I had a LOT to prove. My team was so skeptical about it that, for more than a year, it was an unofficial project with no priority. Whenever I talked about this Key amplifier, my coworkers just rolled their eyes, silently telling me to "just shut up already." This project was "my baby." I worked on it day and night, weekends and holidays. When it was almost finished, one of my colleagues listened to it and said that it was awful, that it sounded like "crap." He didn't have an inch of compassion in the delivery of his criticism. He didn't care that I had worked my butt off, trying so hard to prove myself as a new hire—he just dropped the hammer. Once I got past my hurt feelings, I began thinking about his criticism. I knew that it never sounded like crap, ever! But nonetheless, I started contemplating whether there might be *some truth* to what he said. With my curiosity piqued, I went to the office on an early Sunday and carefully listened to it, playing his role as a fault finder. I truly felt that it was good but could be further improved, and as a result, I spent another week tweaking it to the finest possible audible result. Well, today my Key amplifier is shipping worldwide and getting mostly excellent reviews. By listening to that one criticism from my highly antagonistic colleague, I potentially prevented many dreadful public reviews from actual buyers. The cherry on the pie was that based on the success of it, I asked for a salary raise (Chapter 20) that I received without hesitation—maybe that would not have happened without his criticism.

Criticizing in a non-demeaning and constructive way is just as important as handling criticism well. The weaker the relationship is between you and the person that you are criticizing, the more carefully you need to choose your words in order to build trust rather than break it. One way to build trust is to wrap the criticism in praise—first beginning by saying what is done well, then segueing into what needs to be improved. Ask the person how they might solve the issue. If possible, propose a solution (or a set of solutions) to help with the problem that you see and ask what they think about it. Try to rely on facts rather than just your own opinion, as well as establish a cause-and-effect relationship. As much as you believe you're right, there is a chance that, actually, you may be wrong. Keep that in mind when delivering your criticism.

Be kind about your criticism. Not only will kindness make your critique more palatable if you're indeed right, but in case you are wrong, it will make apologizing much easier and help them to be able to forgive you for your misplaced criticism. With that level of respectful dialogue, you might even find a good future colleague to make your mutual dreams come true.

Here is a quick example: "John, your grades are very impressive! You must have worked hard to get them! However, your math score isn't quite up there with the other great grades yet,[1] but Jay is an excellent tutor and can help you improve it.[2] A bit higher math score can go a long way in helping you get that scholarship! Do you want to try that?"[3] **Analysis:** 1. What John did well first; what needs improving later. 2. Proposed solution. 3. Establishing cause and effect.

Lastly, every single time that you respond well to criticism, you build your positive reputation a little further. The truth is that the default mode for most people is reacting to the critique in a defensive way, which makes the person criticizing want to criticize even more; if you want criticism to stop, you better listen to it well! It takes a good deal of self-control and maturity to keep an open mind while being criticized, and especially, it takes getting past your own pride to implement positive changes based on that. People look up to the few wise ones that can take criticism well—and you can be one of them!

JUMPSTART

Here is a good way to think about criticism: to repair a leaky tire, the repairman inflates it and dunks the tire in a water tank. By doing so, he can see the bubbles coming up from the puncture hole(s) that need to be fixed. Criticism is the same; it shows exactly where the problems lie, so you can fix them to move forward and farther ahead. Good luck!

Chapter 13

4 pages | 5 minutes

Work Ethic

A good work ethic is not optional; it is more important than any skill that you can develop or any talent that you have.

- Work ethic stems from personal integrity and it heavily influences self-esteem.
- You can only work in cooperation with a great team if you have a good work ethic.
- Work ethic is applicable across the board and during all seasons of life.

A person that cultivates a strong work ethic has much better chances of being successful than someone else more talented, but with questionable work practices. To illustrate this, let's imagine that your car has a problem. You take it to the dealership to repair because they have the best tools and the most knowledgeable people. Two days later, you pick up your car and it runs great, but you're hit with a bill of $1000—that was $200 for parts and $800 for eight hours of labor at a rate of $100/hour. Expensive, no?

Intrigued, you watch some YouTube videos of how to fix that very problem, only to find out that there is NO WAY it would require more than two hours of labor. Even with the work well done and your car running fine, you are now frustrated because you paid them for eight hours of work and they only worked two—you've been *ripped off*. Would you take your car back to that dealership?

JUMPSTART

    Two years later, your car has the same problem. This time, you don't want to get ripped off, so you google "car repair shop" and look for reviews that mention HONESTY, delivered ON TIME, fair price, great customer care, etc. You finally narrow down your search to one repair shop with excellent reviews that emphasize the quality of the service and fairness of price. You give it a try, this time the bill runs only $260, $100 for parts and $160 for two hours of labor at a rate of $80/hour. Not only was the repair good and it met your expectations, but upon delivery they also washed your car and fixed the arm rest that was broken without charging any extra for it. How do you feel now? Would you go back to this shop? Would you recommend it to your friends? Not only did they charge a fair price, but they also *over delivered* work. WOW! Did they have better tools or better knowledge than the dealership? No. So what was the major difference? The morale. That's what work ethic means: *work morale*. Your work morale stems from your own personal morale.

    Chances are that you have a job. Out of eight hours a day, how many hours are you committed to it? If your number is on the lower side, then tell me, how are you any different from the dealership that charges for eight hours of labor but works only two?

    Let's say that your boss is mean, that the company you work for stinks and that you're seriously getting underpaid. Should you *underwork* for these reasons? Do all these seemingly unfair factors justify you having a poor work ethic? The thing is, I would never ask you to do your best for a company or someone who's ripping you off and treating you with less dignity than you deserve. But I would SURELY encourage you to do your best for YOU. Don't work hard for them, work hard for YOU.

    You might feel like a fool by doing all that much for an employer that doesn't recognize or compensate you for your efforts and work ethic. I get it. But if you truly want to achieve your goals and work with awesome people, a solid work ethic is a prerequisite. You have to have it; there is no quick fix or working around that. Therefore, it doesn't matter how much your employer disrespects you, how negative your colleagues are, or how much it all seems to pull you in the opposite direction of your goals. Practice work ethic. Incorporate work ethic. Make work ethic something that you take pride in yourself for. Hold yourself up to a high standard of an excellent work ethic and don't change for anything. Make work ethic your constant for the entirety of your life, and not only will you be guaranteed to dig yourself out of any bad situation if you fail and fall, but you will have a real chance at succeeding at your most daring goals.

    Your skills will change. You will learn new things that you find necessary along the way. Other things you've learned will become obsolete and no longer usable. You might switch career paths and disrupt yourself multiple times. With all this change, the only thing that must remain solid and constant is your work ethic. Develop it and keep it, whether you are rich or poor, employed or unemployed, owning your own business or not, etc.

    Work ethic has a great impact on your self-image and self-esteem—it will either build or damage it. If the people you work with have flawed work ethics, set yourself apart by being the different one, and like I said, do it for YOU and not for anyone else.

    You would be surprised at the lengths that your employer will go to in order to keep you around if you have a good work ethic. Likewise, you would be surprised at the lengths that your customers will go to in order to recommend your services and business. The thing is, whether you're an employee or entrepreneur, you are always providing a service; therefore, your employer IS your customer.

    You know what else your employer is? Your investor. If you have a side hustle (Chapter 18), your day job is allowing you to invest and work on your dreams. So why would you screw with it? If you're aspiring to have your own business, treat the company that you work for as if it is your own.

    If your coworkers don't share the work ethics of the successful, chances are, as you evolve and mature your work ethic, they will start to reject you. This will be painful and lonely, but it is okay to *not fit in* with those who don't represent who you want to become—just accept that. Ideally, you will try to lift others around you and inspire them to ride this train with you. Maybe some of them will buy into it and become *running mates* with you! Maybe they won't and will start to resent you. Understand that when you start working better and harder than your coworkers, it will make them look bad—it *exposes* them, both to themselves and to others. Don't take it personally. Keep on it and remember that the road to success is full of inconveniences that will make you grow and mature. If the leader of your group (your boss) has a flawed work ethic himself, do not take on the almost impossible task to change your group's mindset; you may not have enough leverage for that. Instead, use the pain of this very uncomfortable situation as a motivator to find a better path in your career, whether that be a different job with a more motivated work group or your own business.

Your work ethic is right when the people that owe you nothing are happy to pay you. When you get money from complete strangers in exchange for your service, and upon your delivery they have a big smile on their face, that means you're doing it right. Whether you're an employee or business owner, the same applies. Challenge yourself to make strangers happier to pay you each time! This is such a greatly rewarding experience; you truly feel that you've done something well.

My final advice to you is, for every new customer you have, always overdeliver. For recurring customers or your employer, overdeliver every once in a while, to remind them and yourself of your own strong work ethic. Remember that when you do your best work, you're not only serving others but you're serving yourself too. Make an excellent work ethic habitual.

Chapter 14

5 pages | 7 minutes

Leadership at the Workplace

"The bottom line in leadership isn't how far we advance ourselves, but how far we advance others." - John C Maxwell

- The greatest qualities of genuine leaders are selflessness and morale.
- Leaders inspire people; managers organize things.
- Leaders can greatly benefit from management skills, and managers can greatly benefit from leadership skills.
- People must buy into YOU before they buy into your mission.

Even if you are an impressive visionary with incredible skills and a perfect business plan, that will not get others to follow you. In fact, trying to convince people to buy into your mission can do more harm than good. What gets people to follow you isn't how smart, talented, and creative you are, but how much you *care* about people.

Take a deep look inside of yourself and ask whether you genuinely care about others; when you do, it shows, and people will naturally buy into *you*. Only then is the door wide open for you to pitch your vision to them.

Unfortunately, it's not uncommon to see people in leadership positions that will do everything in their power to appear to be strong and smart, trying to hide their weaknesses at all times. Typically, these individuals are quite self-centered and tend to suffocate others' good ideas, afraid of being "outshined." Poor leaders like this won't hesitate to lie and cover up their shortcomings, take credit for other people's work, or worse. An effective leader will not hesitate to admit his or her weaknesses, and to place others that possess the very skills that they lack in strategic positions to perform their best. They prioritize the group and the cause, and their ego takes the backseat. That only begins to scratch the surface of morale in leadership.

A good leader becomes absorbed in the cause. The money, status, and bells and whistles that may come with a leadership position are all secondary. The cause is to lead a group of people towards success, while taking care of each individual in the process. As per Gallup's research (see #1), the four strongest reasons why people follow someone are:

1) **Trust:** honesty, integrity, and respect. Followers that trust their leaders do more things for them and with them.
2) **Compassion:** caring, friendship, happiness, and love. You want them to know that you have their wellbeing as your highest priority.
3) **Stability:** security, strength, support, and peace. People need stability in the short term and security for the long term, meaning that they know that they're not getting fired tomorrow for no good reason.
4) **Hope:** Strong leaders instill hope in the hearts of their followers, especially when crisis hits!

Leaders and managers are completely different animals, and yet, it's best that they possess significant amounts of each other's qualities. Leaders inspire people, while managers organize things.

A leader has the ability to inspire people to *buy into* his or her mission; the team becomes willingly devoted, out of their own desire to be part of it. If this same leader lacks management skills, the inspiration and hopes planted in their hearts can turn into frustration, as the leader fails to organize things to move forward.

A manager that is a good organizer but fails to inspire the team will find great resistance as they won't do anything willingly. Rather, they will only perform the designated work because they "have to."

These uninspiring managers will have a lot of push back from their group, even if they are competent as a manager. As a result, creativity withers away and dismay takes its place. It is extremely frustrating for both the manager and the team. This happens in companies if employees with no leadership skills become managers, simply because they've been there long enough.

The leader's behavior and morale spreads to the group, including work ethics, lifestyle, and even personal care. If your boss is always late for work, you'll probably be getting there late too (unless your work ethic is very strong). If your boss is always the first to arrive and the last to leave, you might also start putting in some extra hours of work yourself without being asked to do so. For better or worse, the team is likely to become a reflection of their leader.

Ask each of your team players two questions. What are they <u>good at</u> **AND** <u>enjoy doing</u> (green zone)? What are they <u>not good at</u> **OR** <u>don't enjoy doing</u> (red zone)? Position as much as possible your players inside the green zone, which is a happy and fertile place to be. Even if you're the nicest boss in the world, positioning your team players in the red zone will make them miserable. Misery is bad business for *you* as the leader because it is guaranteed to bring the lowest returns in terms of productivity.

Don't ask your team players to have a "complementary set of strengths," or worse, to "work on their weaknesses to get better." Instead, hire team members that have different and complementary skills in regard to each other from the start. What is the red-zone for one is the green-zone for another. Balance is achieved as the task that John hates to do is Jane's favorite task. Everyone is happy and the team is productive.

Although the skillset of your team members should be very different, to get along well, it is important that they share commonalities regarding their values and personalities. As a leader, it is <u>your job</u> to put in the time and the effort to make these relationships work. Keep tabs on it. Promote cooperation and defuse adversity or unhealthy competition between team players.

It will often be necessary to sit down with two or more people that aren't getting along well to talk, vent, and figure out how to resolve the little annoyances that are bound to happen when people work together. Instead of waiting for them to come to you with a big problem, try to be the initiator for conflict resolution, because when they finally come to you for help, they may be at their breaking point already. Why wait for that to happen? Be approachable and, in private, give them a safe space to express their feelings and talk things out, without the risk of getting punished or fired.

Publicly praise and recognize their ideas and achievements. Privately give them corrective feedback. Let them try new things and expand their boundaries, even if it means failing sometimes. Don't just sprinkle orders from the top, pay attention to what they like to work on and show appreciation for their initiatives. Always <u>encourage independent thinking that serves the common goal,</u> especially for those that like to innovate. For those that don't have much a mind of their own and need to be led more constantly, offer them a list of things to do and ask them to choose out of the bunch what they want to work on, or at least, let them decide the order in which they will work on things. This way, they will feel more empowered, instead of you trying to dictate them specific orders.

The sooner you realize that you're never going to lose your position because someone does a better job at "xyz" than you, the better. People love those who nurture their talents. That's the kind of boss and ultimately CEO that is respected the most. When you don't understand something that your subordinate is doing, humbly ask him (or her) to explain and demonstrate it to you. Try not to focus on HOW people do their jobs; rather, focus on the outcome of their work. Young people especially crave being evaluated on their results rather than how they go about their tasks, manage their schedules, wear their clothes, etc. As a leader, you can and should hire and nurture the people that can do a better job than you.

The higher up you are, the more you serve. If you're at the bottom of the hierarchical pyramid, you're just told what to do; you perform the designated work, go home, and forget about it. As you rise in position, your team will ask you for pointers and answers to their questions—they need your guidance. Give them what they need first; THEN go about doing your own stuff—serve others first.

Lastly, the leader of a chaotic team is either incompetent or lazy, because simply put, a leader's job is to keep everyone in the canoe paddling in the same direction. Show me how well a team work together, and I'll show you how competent (or not) their boss is.

Remember: They buy into you, then they buy into your mission, and as a result, they cooperate with each other. Can you make that happen?

References:

1. Successful Leadership: The 4 Needs of Followers: https://www.gallup.com/cliftonstrengths/en/334373/successful-leadership-4-needs-followers.aspx

Chapter 15

5 pages | 7 minutes

Using Gratification well

Never underestimate the power of gratification—for both good and bad. Although most people are swayed by gratification in a way that hurts them, you can consciously use it to your advantage.

- You can create savings and improve your finances simply by delaying gratification.
- Delaying gratification increases your mind's resilience and ability to plan long-term.
- Rewarding yourself for your accomplishments keeps you motivated.
- Inability to resist instant or free gratification makes you vulnerable to scams, addictions, and inability to cope with failure.

Let's imagine that you have no significant savings, and that your job only pays the bills. At the same time, you have that ITCH to get a new(er) car, as you simply can't stand driving an old beater any longer. One fine day you get a bit of a raise, and the extra money is just right—not more and not less—to cover for a new car payment. FINALLY, right?! Now you can go get the new car and scratch that itch! Of course, you can.

While there's nothing wrong with that, here's the thing: if you get the new car as soon as you can afford it, it's not bad, but you didn't make any progress in terms of your finances; you're still living paycheck to paycheck, with no savings. However, if you simply **delay** getting this same car for one year, you can add to your savings. Let's assume that the car payment is a reasonable $278. You would accumulate $3,336.00 in savings *and* still get the new car, just a bit later. In the same exact circumstances, if you delay getting the car for three years instead of one, now you'll have 10 grand in savings *and* the car. See my point?

   This is exactly what I lived through: I rode a bike for 5 months upon arriving broke in the U.S., then bought an old VW Jetta for $3,500.00. Although I could afford a nicer car just two years later, I kept driving the Jetta for almost five years. I promised myself that, *when I had X amount of savings,* I would get a new car. I created a **condition** for my gratification, which motivated me to meet it—and believe me, I REALLY wanted a new car.

   Once I met my own condition, I purchased the BMW I wanted (used, but still...) and, although I could afford it outright, I chose to finance it. As I had quite a bit of savings, I didn't worry about selling the old Jetta and ended up renting it out to a friend, which covered part of the BMW payment. As I didn't touch my savings, I was able to put it down as part of a down payment for a "duplex home" property. I could live in one unit and rent out the other unit. As a result, I had the new car, the old car, and a duplex property. The key for all that was simply **waiting** to get the new car—it was as simple as that. Had I purchased the BMW as soon as I could afford it, I would still be living in an apartment, paying rent, and with less savings. It is a great gain in the moment, and it creates greater gain years down the line, as these financial decisions have a compound effect.

   This whole thing about delaying gratification may sound a bit simplistic and uninteresting because it's not a "hidden secret for exponential growth," but remember that small adjustments that you make **early**, have an enormous impact on your long-term success because it *snowballs*. Maybe a bit of money that you save up by delaying some gratifications can be the seed of a profitable business of your own, or allow you to make a profitable investment, or at minimum, save your butt on a rainy day—if you lose your job, for example. The great deal on the duplex property came about unexpectedly, but when it did, I had the money to seize the opportunity. Like they say, "Luck is when preparation meets opportunity." As you've seen with the history of Ray (addendum to Chapter 8), it doesn't matter that you don't know yet what you'll be doing in the future, because having savings opens the door for whatever you choose to do next. Once you figure that out, you already have the cash to start it.

Unfortunately, the way most people go about gratifying themselves destroys their future, and often, their *character* as a person. Take "happy hour" for instance; many people go to "happy hour" as often as they can, spending several dollars repeatedly, regardless of how their finances are doing. Even when they have had a really sloppy and unproductive day, they *still* go. What if you apply a **condition** on attending happy hour? <u>If and when</u> you really do well on your goals, then you go. For example, if your health is on point and you just had a great day at work, then you go to happy hour to *celebrate* it—that feels more meaningful, it feeds your soul! This small adjustment, over the years, may be the difference between becoming an alcoholic in debt, OR becoming a happy, healthy and genuinely successful person that *occasionally* likes to "tear it up" at the bar.

Remember that this sort of thing is cumulative, and therefore, no, it's not okay to do even more of what is already hurting you. Ideally, you want to completely stop doing anything that further aggravates the issues you're working hard to overcome. Although stopping detrimental habits cold turkey is generally difficult, it's necessary to reduce it enough to build intensity and momentum in your progress. For example, if you're on a mission to save money or lose weight, it's important that you follow through with enough diligence to be proud of yourself and actually see results.

We all slip up every once in a while, and that's not the end of the world, as long as that is the *exception* and not the norm. Forgive yourself for the past and get right back into the mindset for the future. It's a mistake to think that we cheat on our promises, when in fact, we're cheating on *ourselves*—but feeling guilty doesn't help. Like everyone else, I too slip up sometimes! When I do, I compensate for it if necessary, and you too can employ the same tactic.

A life of pure sacrifice without any gratification is a sad way to live. I don't like living frugally, but even more so, I *hate* to put my future in jeopardy. We ought to enjoy what life has to offer us in terms of places, possessions, travel, social gatherings, and deliciously calorie-rich foods. However, before letting your urge for gratification and instant relief guide you, stop and ask yourself, "Can I afford to do or to buy what I want with no harm?" If the answer is a solid YES, go for it! <u>It's a balance of restraint and indulgence</u>, you want to not only keep that balance in check, but you also want to have **control** over it. You cannot live *for* gratification—you have to own it, instead of letting it own you!

You can and should reward yourself when you do well—it will **motivate you**. The opposite, however, will spoil you. If you teach yourself that you can have nice things and travel to cool places in spite of not doing well, you will be even less motivated to work towards being successful, and eventually, it may get you in trouble, in debt, and in a downward spiral. Remember, it's cumulative!

When you **earn** your gratification, it *feels* different. Having a beer knowing that there's a pile of work to be done doesn't feel quite as good as having the same beer **because** you successfully got through that entire pile of work. The same goes for traveling to places and buying things. For instance, in that initial example of delaying the purchase of a car to build up some savings first, I can guarantee that the more you delay purchasing it, the happier you'll be when you finally get to drive it! In that case, if you commit to buying the car you want *only when you have X amount of savings*, you'll be much better off, not only with your money, but also with how you feel about yourself and even how happy you will be when you finally drive your new car.

By delaying gratification, you exercise and create the ability to plan long-term; you want to get to the point that you have no problem with a five or even ten-year plan. In fact, you might actually enjoy the idea of seeing father into the future. On the contrary, if you *give in* to every kind of gratification that you can immediately indulge, such as the "likes" on social media, food, alcohol, porn, or buying things you don't need, you become unable to make any sort of long-term plan because you "gotta have it now." You don't build a life truly worth living that way—it takes work, it takes patience, it takes perseverance. How many people want to be their own boss? A bunch. How many people have the resilience to keep fighting for two, three, five years—or more—until their business finally makes a profit? Not so many. In a world of videogames, pornography, online shopping, social media, and highly processed foods with loads of added sugar, the people able to resist instant gratification are few and far between. Most people don't even realize how they're basically being manipulated by businesses that don't care whether you become healthy and wealthy or ill and broke.

    Delaying gratification makes you more resilient and able to follow through with your long-term goals (chapter 08) because you have prepared yourself to do so. When your mind adjusts for long-term reward, you become immune to the scams and addictions that are on every corner, such as drugs and addictive foods, as well as schemes such as "get rich quick," and "miracle diet" programs. Better yet, you immediately conserve the time and money that you would have spent towards those notoriously unsuccessful activities. A person that thinks short-term sees failure (chapter 11) as a dead end, whereas a person who thinks long-term sees failure simply as a road bump—it's a pivotal difference.

    Strangely as it seems, you can find gratification in delaying gratification! For example, you can feel proud of yourself for not spending money buying something you would normally buy on an impulse. When I first lost weight at the age of 18, I immediately felt good about eating only two slices of pizza and leaving the other 6 alone. I felt that I had control and trusted myself more. Delaying gratification does wonders for the *reputation you have with yourself,* a.k.a., self-esteem (chapter 6).

Chapter 16

8 pages | 11 minutes

How to become UNSTOPPABLE

Find out EXACTLY WHY you're on a mission. Is that mission making money, losing weight, having your own business, getting married to the right person, or something else? Associate excellent reasons to accomplish your goals, and you will be sure to follow through with them.

- For everything you do, ask yourself why you're doing it.
- Problems will look insignificant compared to how important your mission is.
- It's hard NOT to put in the work and effort required when you know WHY you're doing it.

By the end of 2011, my self-esteem was low and my hopes for the future were dim. I felt that I was hermetically sealed away from any chances of success. Simply being able to pay the bills sounded amazing, yet impossible, to me. After five years of incessant grinding as an entrepreneur, there I was without a degree, in debt, out of shape, and living with "mommy" in Brazil. I moved all my tools and furniture out of the much loved office that I had rented for my business initiative and into my tiny bedroom. That was the crack in the dam. I now was sleeping between two workbenches, the underside of my bed and my dresser were filled with parts and tools, and I had no income. To top it all off, my upstairs neighbor compulsively dragged furniture almost every morning, and downstairs was a shop that would grind metal all day long. My quality of life was such that I simply did not want to wake up to live another day like that.

To make things worse, I realized that I was already becoming obsolete in the field that I had chosen—of audio—because there was a new technology called digital signal processing (DSP) revolutionizing the industry, and I didn't have a grip on it at all. In fact, I didn't even have the resources to do so: learning DSP required a level of calculus far beyond my very basic math capabilities at that time. I figured that the best I could do was to take a "few" steps back to plug the mathematical hole in my academic education—a whole bunch of steps, actually.

Consequently, I tried to apply for a scholarship at the University of Miami (UM) using my real-world achievements in audio electronics, by showing the products that I had designed and manufactured in Brazil. I wanted it so badly that I travelled from Brazil to Miami, rented an Airbnb in Little Haiti, and roamed around the UM campus for an entire month like a beggar, showing the StudioMotion to teachers and deans of colleges in hopes of obtaining that scholarship. Most of them were really impressed, but none of them would accept me as a student—not even if I paid full tuition! It seemed that I was finally paying the price for being a sloppy student most of my academic life. I was exhausted and stuck.

After this disappointing and money-wasting trip to UM, I came back to Brazil with a bunch of DSP books. I tried to read them, but I couldn't understand much of it because I was simply unable to follow the calculus. I felt very ignorant. Clearly, I needed help, so I looked for a calculus tutor on the internet and found professor Marcio Vieira. I explained my situation to him: "these are the books I need to read. Please tell me what I need to learn first, to be able to make sense of them." In turn, he asked me, "First, what do you know?" I knew middle school math and not much else. I basically needed high-school math plus a minimum of four years of college put together, but I could only afford to pay Marcio for six months. Marcio very respectfully told me that it was too much of a gap to fill in such a short time frame, but his facial expression was actually telling me: "You gotta be out of your f*cking mind dude!"

We agreed that as long as I paid him, he would keep showing up, even though the problem was too big and he was no miracle worker. So we began. I SPARED NO EFFORTS to learn what I needed to learn in order to accomplish what I had in mind. In fact, Marcio thoroughly enjoyed teaching me because I was really working my ass off. He even told me, "If I win the lottery, I will quit teaching everyone, and I will teach you for free!" That was incredible to hear, especially because I was a lousy student most of my life in school.

Well, we accomplished the seemingly impossible: more than four years of formal education shrunk into six short months. Marcio himself called it a "Herculean task." Having mastered calculus to a sufficient degree, I could finally understand the DSP books that seemed encrypted to me before.

As a result, I came up with a new idea for a DSP-based, high value car-audio product that I initially believed to be *way* out of my wheelhouse. But, I was determined to do whatever necessary to accomplish it. I read the DSP books focused like a laser beam and immediately applied the lessons learned by building yet another piece of my [Audiosigma DSP](#) project.

By the end of 2013, I finished the project and saw it selling in a few stores in Brazil. Not only had I learned DSP in two years without paying 38k/year in tuition fees to UM, but I had a real-world product ready to manufacture and SELL. Today, my latest DSP product is the Award Winning [Kicker KEY amplifier](#) that sells world-wide. In July of 2021, I was granted the patent #US 10,979,847 for my own DSP algorithm featured in the KEY amp!

In theory, (a) not having a degree would stop me from learning DSP, (b) making the [Audiosigma DSP](#) would require an army of formally educated engineers, (c) being depressed and hating every minute spent in that bedroom would keep me feeling too emotionally exhausted to put effort into changing my destiny. Yet, I made it through, in spite of all that. So, what kept me going in the worst moments? What made me UNSTOPPABLE? The answer is simple. <u>As long as I kept going, I had hope.</u> The more I dedicated myself to the studies and the work I was doing, the more I could see a better future. This was my thought process: study calculus to read the DSP books; read the DSP books to design a product; design a product to change my life.

I made the DECISION THAT MY LIFE WOULD NOT SUCK, and that made me UNSTOPPABLE. Lisa Nichols became UNSTOPPABLE after wrapping her eight-month-old baby in a towel because she was unable to afford diapers. Right there and then, she decided that she would never be broke again, so her son could have a bright future. She's a millionaire now. Jim Carrey became UNSTOPPABLE when he saw his father broken and down on his knees after getting fired from his much-hated job as an accountant—a job he bared only to pay the bills, at the expense of his dream of being a saxophonist. Carrey decided that he would never allow himself to end up like his father. He realized that if you can fail at something you only bear to do in order to make ends meet, you might as well risk failing at what you love doing, so he went on to pursue his career as an actor and became successful.

The greatest gift you can possibly give yourself is an excellent reason to become successful at what you love doing. Spend the time required to figure out the WHY to your life. Meditate on it, pray about it, and sleep on it! Ponder it as you eat, drink, exercise, and go about your day. For everything you do in life, connect a strong WHY to it. Once you do, you, too, are UNSTOPPABLE.

At the time of this writing, I work a full-time job at Kicker and, at the same time, on another three projects. I'm choosing to live a rather modest life, so that I can set aside 30% of my income to invest. These other projects are hard, time consuming and they may or may not bring me a monetary return; but if they do, I will use it to further invest. If these projects don't bring a monetary return, I will come up with new, different projects and continue to march forward in the same direction. The goal is to solve for money, so that I can run my own business out of love, not necessity. This love will trickle down to each and every person for whom I hope to earn the opportunity to provide a job.

Even though I have all these reasons WHY, it's still not easy to wake up much earlier to work on my side-hustle (chapter 18) before getting to my normal job obligations early in the morning. But it becomes REALLY HARD not to do it. I have a friend to whom I can't wait to give something amazing to sell. Then, he can make his own money with it, and I can consequently see him living well and being able to put his son through private school in Brazil, as public schools there are an educational death sentence. His family is one of my WHY reasons.

If I fail to push my projects forward, I would be failing my future employees. I would be failing people that can benefit from the words I'm typing in this book. I would be failing people that need food to eat and clothes to wear. My WHY is not about me anymore; it's bigger than me. Now I am UNSTOPPABLE because I cannot fail the dozens, hundreds, maybe thousands of people that I may benefit directly or indirectly if I follow through with my dreams. It's impossible to ignore all of them and just sit contentedly because I can pay my own bills. That's not enough. Give yourself excellent reasons to become successful and join me in NOT LETTING GO OF OUR DREAMS!

--

Let's change gears. Are you *pumped* with motivation? If you are, great. If you are not, also great. Here is the truth about working on your dreams: while you can certainly *increase or decrease* the odds of it becoming a reality, from zero by not taking action (Chapter 10), to good by working consistently on it, you can't know for sure whether they will come true or not. But, still, *working on your dreams is always the best option*, regardless of the outcome.

Understanding this, is the difference between working on them "on and off," which normally ends nowhere, or being consistent in

JUMPSTART

your efforts even when motivation is low. When you do it for the *work itself* rather than an ideal outcome that may or may not ever happen, paradoxically, you increase the odds of attaining the result you want. In other words, to achieve your dreams, do it for work, not for the result. When you do that and someone says to your face, "You'll never get there," you can simply laugh it off because you're in it for the process, not for the aftermath. This way, even if you have doubts as to whether you'll achieve your dreams or not, you *still* won't stop working on them. THAT is bullet proof, my friend. Let's look at the reasons to take this approach.

1. Skillset and value: When you work on your dreams for the future, you develop and grow your skills — sooner or later, they will serve you well. Although I wasn't successful with the company I started at the age of 18 in Brazil, the skills acquired in the pursuit of being a world-class developer of audio products led me to become a permanent resident of the U.S. at the age of 31 with an excellent job in that field. If my current job is the intermediate step to my dream, then I'm paying the bills with the profits of the *pursuit* itself.

Have I achieved my dream yet? No. Have I benefited from the *pursuit* of it? Absolutely. Will I ever stop this pursuit? No. I know that either I will have my own audio company, or I'll die trying. All the while, I keep pushing in the original direction with my side-hustle (chapter 18).

2. Fabrication of hope: When you work on your future, you create the hope — and the possibility — of having a better life, which makes your present time brighter or at least more bearable. Hope and quality of life are intrinsically connected. For example, if you're unemployed or stuck with a job that is chipping away at your zest for life, just by making your moves towards the future that you desire will immediately improve your spirits, because that creates a sense of *perspective*. Therefore, making these moves are, in and of itself, worthwhile just for how it makes you feel.

As long as you have **hope and health**, both of which you have much control over, you can get through most anything. In fact, hope is so powerful that it actually improves your health — you may confirm that by reading the histories of cancer or Holocaust survivors. For this reason, work on your dreams, not for the potential benefits in a far out future, but for the immediate improvement in your present time.

3. Pain shapes us: While working on your dreams is likely to make your future better, it doesn't mean that you won't have to endure pain in the process. Whether you're leaving it to chance or being proactive about it, life will throw curve balls at you. The difference is that, when times get hard, it's unquestionably better to endure what you chose, than what you didn't. The pain of the struggle is pretty much always guaranteed, for everyone. This pain shapes our character, changes our behavior, how we see the world, and even how we relate to other people.

If pain is guaranteed, the remaining question is: would you prefer to be shaped by the pain that *you chose,* or by the pain that just sort of *happened* to you? Well, my reasoning is, "If it's going to shape me, then I'll be damned if I don't choose it myself." If you, too, don't like the idea of being shaped by hardships that "just randomly happen," then working on your future is better than leaving it to chance.

Lastly, we need to ditch the word "dream" and replace it with the word "future." The very word "dream" denotes the attachment to an *ideal outcome* that must happen within an *ideal timeframe*. "Ideal" is demotivating, because chances of things happening exactly the way we want are very slim—and we know it. The word "future" denotes the *inevitable*; as long as we're breathing, it will happen whether we want it or not. However, it is up to us to work on it in advance, so that when it comes, it has a higher chance of looking something like our "dream." With all that in mind, let's do some myth-busting about working on your dreams:

Truths:
- It's within your power to increase or decrease the odds of your dreams becoming true.
- Hope improves the quality of your life.
- Working on your dreams for the future makes your present better, regardless of the outcome.
- Even if your dreams don't come true, by working on them, your future will still be best aligned with your goals and values.
- Pain is inevitable. By working on your future, at least you get to choose the pains that will shape you.

Lies:
- Working on your dreams is a waste if it doesn't end up becoming a reality.
- You have to be extremely intelligent or very lucky for your dreams to come true.
- Life is easier if you don't follow your dreams.
- You can avoid failure by having more "mundane" goals and careers.

Like many people, I don't always feel optimistic about my dreams becoming my reality, and I do not deny the uncertainty of it. But what keeps me going in this direction is what working on my future does for my present: I feel better, I feel happier, I feel more fulfilled. I'm in it for the process, not for the reward. When your motivation fails, remember that *working on your dreams is always the best choice*, both for both your present and future—and that makes you *unstoppable*.

Chapter 17

6 pages | 10 minutes

Unlocking the Power of Your Mind

"I measure my accomplishments not by how tired I am at the end of the day, but how tired I am not." - Daniel W. Josselyn
- Multitasking is a myth. Having a variety of tasks at hand can make or break your performance depending on how you handle them.
- It's easier to direct and lock-in your focus upon waking up rather than later in the day.
- Going back to a task is easier than getting to start doing it.
- Meditation and Power naps replenish the mind and boost your focus and mental energy.

While we can only do one thing at a time, having just a single task at hand for too long can get boring. Conversely, switching over to different tasks too frequently gets overwhelming, as you spread yourself thin and most likely will end up having a busy but not quite productive day. However, this does vary greatly from person to person. For example, an executive assistant may be comfortable switching over different tasks and re-focusing on what needs to be done, while a software engineer may not get bored coding the same thing for hours on end. The question is, what works best for you?

I believe that there are a great number of people that are not on either extreme, and perhaps, having exactly two different things at your disposal that you can work on at any given time, may be helpful. Having two tasks avoids the boredom of a single heavy lifting, while not being enough to overwhelm with "multitasking."

JUMPSTART

This way, you have the opportunity to switch over to a different task just before you get bored with what is currently at hand, then go back to it moments later—if you wish to do so. For example, when I was coding iOS apps, I would work on the code until I sensed that I was approaching being mentally tired, then before I started to rub my face, I would switch over to the design elements such as the icons, background pictures, etc. After designing the artistic elements for a while and just as the fun started to fade, I would switch over back to coding the back end of the app. Both parts of the app needed to be done, that being code and design, and alternating between them when I felt like it helped me accomplish the work without burnout.

The two different tasks don't need to be related, necessarily. Another example is, if you're doing schoolwork, you can from time to time go wash a couple of plates, play an instrument, or do some exercise! The whole point is to not get bored or burn out; break out of it before you start dozing off or overheating your mind.

I am in no shape or form promoting multitasking. First of all, it's a myth. No one can multitask, some may be more skilled at jumping between different tasks than others, but every single human is only able to tackle one executive function at a time—this is a limitation of your prefrontal cortex. With that in mind, to perform your best, you must switch between tasks when the time is right. Squeezing your brain to get one more drop of juice out of it "kinda works" short term, but it will burn you out and take away all the joy from work. That's how you block creativity. On the contrary, stopping what you're doing while you're flowing nicely because "something else came up" also will have a negative effect — like sex, if you're in the mood and pause to do something else, there's no guarantee that you'll still be in the mood for it after.

Whenever you're working with a group of people, others can come to you with questions or requests. Unless urgent, work until you get a little tired, then answer other people's requests when you need to take a break. Usually work cycles are between 30 minutes to two hours—depending on your attention span—, and quite frankly, most people can wait that long to get their requests answered. If you drop everything you're doing just because someone asks you to do something for them, you'll be hurting your productivity, while encouraging others to interrupt you frequently. That's why it's not uncommon to see someone who has a people-pleasing personality getting abused in work settings. Don't enable that behavior and guard your productivity.

Just like you want to time answering other people's requests, you also want to time answering your own requests. When a thought comes up, such as "need to call the doctor," write it down and get to it when your work cycle ends. Needless to say, while you're on a productive cycle, keep your phone silent and close all social media and emails. You can always check it, but don't let it interrupt you. You can and should still do right by others, just not immediately. In sum, preserve the flow.

Speaking of attention span, I know that often it is hard to keep your focus on the task at hand, especially if you have some degree of attention deficit. A good remedy for it is setting a timer—you can use your phone for that. I'd recommend a minimum of 30 minutes. It's easier to sit still and do what needs to be done when you know the alarm will go off quite soon, and you voluntarily chose that time limit. Challenge yourself to gradually increase this focus time.

Because work can get boring, you can also leverage switching over activities that are very different in nature as a form of introducing variety in your day, this way, replenishing your spirits. For example, switching from studying to writing an email does not have the same replenishing benefit as switching from studying to exercising. Different parts of the brain need different forms of nurturing! It's important that you practice being present during these activities, whether that is working out or writing a dissertation. Use this type of diversification to maintain and advance different aspects of your life, such as health and social pillars (Chapter 27).

Although it's great to organize yourself with time-blocks, it's perhaps even better to organize your day and activities by sections that

JUMPSTART

you can start and finish. For example, if I make the determination that I will write or read one hour in the morning before getting to my other activities, I shouldn't stop and move away from it as soon as the predetermined 60 minutes are up, but rather, as soon as I finish the chapter or paragraph that I am working through. I call it "closing that box."

The key is to avoid getting back to unfinished things as much as possible and turning to a new page every time you come back to it; I personally apply it in most aspects of my life, including conversations, everyday to-do lists, engineering work, etc.

As I am someone who has a fairly high degree of anxiety and a pretty short attention span, and for this reason, I love to use the morning focus. As you wake up, your brain is slow. Consequently, it is much easier to intentionally direct your mental focus to what is most important, before a million thoughts start to emerge. During the first hour that you are awake, avoid distractions and get started on the most meaningful task of the day that requires mental work. This will lock in your focus. The benefit of working just a few minutes first thing upon waking up is quite astounding. I often sleep with a bottle of water by the bedside, so as soon as I wake up, I drink that water and pop open my laptop to start working. It's amazing how much you can accomplish little by little like that. Instead of reaching for the snooze button, you may want to reach to your side-hustle (chapter 18) instead!

Sure, you will need to stop for breakfast, shower, etc. But going back to what you were doing before is much easier than finally getting started to do it later in the day. Example: Wake up and work on that complicated business proposal for a few minutes. Stop to shower, eat and drive to the office. Upon arriving, you're GOING BACK to working that proposal, instead of cold starting it. In this case, you purposely left the "business proposal box open" during the inevitable pause between working upon waking up and arriving at the office, in order to hit the ground running when you arrive. Beyond that, the shower and drive time are equally valuable for you to process it in your mind; you may be driving and suddenly a light bulb goes off in your head, as you have an exciting idea about what you were doing! By creating this habit, ideas will come to you more frequently.

So, when should you leave a box open, and when should you close it? Well, that is something only you can determine! What works well for me and may work well for you is: when you wake up, open the most important box, work on it, and leave it open. Go do your things, shower, breakfast, etc., then go back to that open box and continue to work on it until you're happy with your progress for the day, then close it. Now, for every other box you open throughout the day, make sure you close them as soon as conveniently possible, avoiding procrastination. Another rule of the thumb is that, when it comes to creative work, it is good to leave that box open and go do other things. Quite often, great ideas emerge not when you're forcefully trying to have them, but when you have the right context active in the background of your mind—that is like fertile ground for ideas to flourish. On the flip side, for work that requires repetition or a specific process, you're always best opening that box, working through it, then closing it before the end of the day. That helps you "get stuff done" and feel more accomplished.

Much of what I describe here I applied in writing this book alongside my full-time job. Upon waking up, I would open the "book writing box," and write anywhere from 10 minutes to one hour. Then, I'd leave that box open and go shower, drive, and have breakfast. During that interval, I was thinking about what I wrote and what I wanted to write. When I did go back to that open box, I found myself creative and productive again, so I wrote some more. Once I was happy with how much I wrote, I closed that box until the next day. After closing the "book writing box," I opened the "job box" and worked on it until I reached a stopping point, always closing it by the end of the day, so I could go to bed with my mind clear.

As we go through the day, our minds collect clutter; advertising, hallway conversations, push notifications on the phone, and a million other forms of distractions—we live in a world of information

JUMPSTART

overload. Because we almost inevitably will get our brains polluted throughout the day, it is important that you use the first few hours of the day to solve the most difficult problems and do creative work. Some people are night owls and would prefer to burn the midnight oil to do that when everything is calm—that is fine too if that works best for you. Use your most productive and creative hours wisely, and once you've already won the day, then you go about doing the other stuff like groceries, cleaning up the house, cooking, and the normal chores, because you don't need a fresh brain for that.

On that note, you can also use other tools to clear up your mind and unleash more of your calm mind power. Particularly meditation and power naps. I am a terrible meditator, so I cannot advise on that, but 15 to 30 minute naps are an efficient way to declutter your mind and reset your stress level. It washes away the stress, dumps the clutter, and brings back the focus and disposition. It is especially helpful for the 40 million people in the U.S. who have sleep disorders such as insomnia, narcolepsy or apnea. Sadly, this is considered unacceptable behavior in many supervised work environments. When working in the office during commercial hours, I would bring my lunch and eat there, then leave for a "lunch break" that instead I used to take a much needed nap—maybe that's a way you can take a nap in the middle of the day, without being frowned upon.

Lastly, for everything you do, be conscious about getting the best return on your time, thought and effort investments. Once you've done *enough and a little extra*, further investing yourself is, in most cases, noth worth it. This applies across the board, from house cleaning to software coding. Many people tend to burn themselves out improving what doesn't need any more improvement—do your best to not overthink or overdo anything that is more than good enough already.

Chapter 18

4.5 pages | 6 minutes

SIDE HUSTLE!

A candid note: this chapter was written at the peak of my pain—and it shows. The first three years working for Kicker were difficult and frustrating. Thanks to Kollin Hodges—a new hire that took over the leadership—, this situation improved completely, and today I thoroughly enjoy my full-time job there.

Do you feel like you can *be more*, and your job actually forces you to *be less*? Then you need a side-hustle (SH)! Living below your true potential is one of the most miserable experiences in life. If you can't afford to quit your job just yet, an SH is the answer.

- An SH should require just two or three hours per working day and some weekend time.
- Your SH must be what you love to do, create value, and have long-term potential.
- Optimism, hope, and a better mood are immediate benefits of a proper SH.
- Coordinate your SH with the time of the day that you feel your best.
- Your SH might even make you better at your regular job.

When we have a full-time job, we feel like we don't have time for any other form of work. It gets worse when you don't like your job as the frustration sucks the life out of you. Don't worry. Putting about two hours a day on your SH should be enough. But don't just put "any" two hours, put your BEST two hours. For most people, two hours in the morning are infinitely better than the same two hours at the end of the day when you're tired and worn out; it sets the mood and the pace for the day. These two hours are your best resource and perhaps the ticket for you to live a much better life. You can keep giving these precious two hours to the traffic commute, to lame co-workers, to an unappreciative boss, OR you can give them to YOURSELF and make some real progress in life.

I am speaking from experience. For 10 years, I had the privilege to be my own boss and chose whatever I wanted to do with my time. My money was short, I worked like a horse, but my feeling of certainty of a successful future was unshakeable. I felt fulfilled. However, after failing miserably with my entrepreneurship adventure in Brazil, I hit rock bottom and HAD to get a job. After that, I did nothing but my job for the first two and a half years, and it was so frustrating that my health started to fail. I hated every day. I was giving away my LIFE—quite literally—in exchange for a paycheck that, before getting a raise, wasn't great at all. I was doing engineer work, but my salary was set by the government as a "technician" because I don't have a degree. It was only after obtaining the Green Card that I could be paid according to the work as engineer that I was performing.

Thanks to my cubicle-working-induced gastritis, I had severe erosive esophagitis. My job was forcing me to be "more"—more mediocre, more complacent, more apathetic, more afraid to be myself. I was getting punished for trying to improve processes and do things better. The endless Monday through Friday cycle of misery, and the I-am-a-victim attitude of some of my co-workers (that eventually got fired) slowly infiltrating through my cracks, started to destroy my hopes of being something more than just mediocre. Funny, as a failing entrepreneur in Brazil I had higher hopes of a brilliant future, than as an employee in America—I did not see that coming. The moment my hopes started to fade, depression started to set in. I could not afford to leave my job, but even more, I realized that I could not afford to lose my hopes. I had no choice but to start an SH that would <u>bring back</u>

my hopes and, given enough time, would hopefully open up the doors to a live worth living. I would do the obvious: work my regular job the entire day, get home feeling like a bag of potatoes, and try to carve out some energy to invest in my SH. Didn't work. At 5:00 pm I was finished, my friend! My mind was foggy, my body was heavy, and I was wrapped in a black cloud of anger and frustration. I was emotionally and spiritually drained. I had a promising SH that I was unable to dedicate myself to, and as a result, it made things worse. I was declining in performance and motivation at my job. I could foresee myself getting fired from the very job I wanted to quit but that was the lifeline to keep the bills paid. Thanks to the "glory loophole," this didn't happen.

The glory loophole: after getting sick and losing 10 pounds in a week, I decided to put my SH first and my job second. I did not quit my job; instead, I dedicated the first two hours of the day to my SH, and only then did I start on my job obligations. I thought that, by doing so, this would take away some of my dedication to my job. **I was wrong**. While previously I would resent my job duties and resist doing them, by beginning the day with my SH that I hold dear to myself, the opposite happened: Whenever I switched from my SH to my job duties, I happily did them. Somehow, I was happy to work for *them* if I worked for *myself* first.

As a result, not only did my SH evolve gloriously, but I also performed great at my job, devoid of all that frustration. The focus and excitement generated by my morning SH would trickle over to my job duties. Moreover, I could see my job as my SH enabler, as a steppingstone rather than a stone over my head. Who would have guessed? The excitement you build in the morning with your SH carries over throughout the day and shields you from frustration and hopelessness. Also, if you can, keep your SH handy. If you have some free time during your working hours, you can switch back and forth between your SH and your regular duties.

Your brain is a machine that loves to associate things. That's how superstition is created; if you see a black cat and you get a flat tire immediately after, your brain associates "black cat = flat tire = bad luck." You can use this inevitable association to your advantage. It doesn't matter that you love your SH if, by the time you get to it, you're in a bad mood and don't want to do it. If you only work on your SH at the end of the day when you're tired, pretty soon you'll no longer love your SH. Your goal is to associate "SH = feeling great" in your brain. For this reason, it's vital that you have a good experience doing it. If you already have your regular job to make you miserable, you don't need your SH to do the same!

But if you only do your SH when you feel good, then you can't be consistent, can you? Yes, you can. In the morning, you set your mood. Wake up earlier, play the music you love, make yourself some delicious coffee, and get to your SH. There's a wonderful sense of "I am in charge" when you do that. Maybe during the day your boss will be a real jerk to you, maybe you'll have a disagreement with a coworker and step on dog poop leaving the office; you never know! But hey, you got that cool side hustle dialed in. It doesn't matter if the rest of the day goes sideways; you won it already. Besides that, during the weekends you will have the choice: "be a couch potato" or "work for myself doing what I love." Chances are, you will often choose to work. When you add up your SH hours Monday through Friday and some more on the weekends, you'll see that it's a pretty significant amount. These are not only "hours;" these are your BEST hours. "It's not the hours you put in your work that count; it's the work you put in the hours." - Sam Ewing.

A proper SH will <u>create value (Chapter 23).</u> It makes you feel good by giving an outlet to your creativity, allowing you to do what you've always wanted to do and perhaps never had a chance. It's not a burden; it's LIBERATING. Examples of SHs include YouTube content, book writing, software coding, creation of products and services, etc. When you work on your dreams first thing in the morning, you will feel like you've done right by yourself and you're no longer getting beat by *the system*. Be 100% sure that you will only work to the best of your abilities when you do what you love to do. You can force yourself to do a less noble SH just to make a buck, like Uber driving, but then, that's it; you're making a buck and not building a future. You're not creating value either. You can't Uber drive your way to wealth; but you definitely can Uber drive your way to exhaustion!

What kind of work would you do even if you won the lottery tomorrow? What is the work that you find pleasurable and you're naturally good at? The author Simon Sinek has put a lot of effort into answering these questions with his books <u>Start With Why</u> and <u>Find Your Why</u>. Every night before you go to bed, ask yourself and sleep on this question: "What is my life's work?" You can also start looking for possible SH ideas at <u>www.udemy.com</u>. Find a program that you like and Take Action (Chapter 10)!

Chapter 19

6 pages | 8 minutes

The "Nine to Five" Job

A 9-to-5 job may be heaven or hell on earth. Consider the culture of the company as well as of your working group. Make sure that you get the position that fits your personality.

- If you are naturally a leader, advertise yourself as such when looking for a job.
- A vocational test can be very helpful whether you think you know what you would like to study and work with, or not.
- Your boss is not the one who pays your salary; it's the end customer that does.
- Watch out for supervisors with a narcissistic personality.
- You can keep growing in the same company by getting transferred to different departments and playing different roles, thereby learning new skills.

Whether you feel like you know exactly what you would like to work with or have no idea what career path to pursue, it is always a good idea to take a vocational test. In case you already know what you love to work with, you can check and ensure that it is indeed aligned with your personality traits and values. A lot of times you may be surprised! If you don't have that clarity yet, then a vocational test is even more helpful for obvious reasons. It's also a great idea to take a vocational test in case you would like to start pursuing a higher education or go back to school.

Why would you want to take a vocational test if you're "pretty damn sure" about what you want to work with or study? For a variety of reasons. You may not know what you really want, even though you think you do. If when you were little your parents enrolled you in a language school to learn German and you did amazingly well, in your adult life you may think you want to be a German teacher or translator; however, this choice wasn't really yours, was it? It was decided for you, before you could decide for yourself. You never questioned it, you never felt the need to question it. Why question what you love, or at least think you do?

In cases like that, which are not uncommon, there may be better fitting career paths for you that you never even thought about. Taking a vocational test may be very revealing, even for the people that are really "sure " about what they would like to pursue. It's YOUR right, your decision, your life, my friend. The sooner you unveil that, the better. Ultimately you want your work to match your personality well, and therefore, be emotionally fulfilling.

I've taken the [Truity - Career Personality Profiler](#) and liked it. Although I'm an exceedingly good electronics engineer, I could, for example, do well as a sales manager (according to the test). As I grew up in a hostile emotional environment, I sheltered myself in electronics, effectively overdeveloping that skill. Success fuels passion, and therefore I found myself in love with electronics. However, working with it in a non-managerial position is not well aligned with my mostly humanitarian and vocal personality—I mean, it's a pretty terrible match, really. Understanding that, you bet that I will investigate other career possibilities, inside and outside Kicker—as I describe in Chapter 25 - Disrupt Yourself.

With that basic concept covered, let's now focus on the two major personality groups; leading and non-leading. Companies have more non-leadership than leadership positions, in other words, more subordinates than bosses—obviously. For this reason, if you are happy in a non-leadership position, you should have plenty of good opportunities to work as an employee. Conversely, if you are a leader, you may need to dig deeper to find a position that allows you to use and grow your leadership skills, rather than stifle them.

There is a huge misconception about who pays your salary. Usually, employees feel that they work for their boss and get paid by them. If your boss / supervisor has a flawed personality, he (or she) may even throw this on your face, as it already happened to me. The truth is that everyone in a company—including the CEO—works for the end customer. Likewise, it is the end customer who pays everyone's salary. It is a single team with a single goal: to provide the customer with the best possible service.

Companies have a power hierarchy in order to keep things organized. By *hierarchy*, I mean president, vice-president, managers, subordinates, etc. The most successful companies have a holistic culture of "we're all in this together." That is, although the hierarchy is in place, it doesn't feel divided into "higher ups" and "lower downs" that much. People treat each other with respect and equality. Ideas for new products, services, and problem resolutions flow in both directions, from the top down and from the bottom up. Leaders take care of their subordinates, serving them the best they can to make sure stress is removed from their lives at work and that they have everything they need to work to the best of their abilities. This is what a great company culture looks like! You can have the time of your life working at companies like Southwest Airlines, LinkedIn, Facebook, and Google, for example.

At the other end of the stick, there are companies with poor culture in which the leaders think they are there to be served and to *boss around*, possibly even bullying their employees. In fact, a company may even have good culture and values, but a particular subgroup of that company may have this rather ill culture. This makes the hierarchy painfully clear, making lower-level employees feel *less* important or less valued than their supervisor. Usually high self-esteem, high performance individuals flee from these companies. Then only the ones that lack confidence or don't have the means to leave, end up staying. Sounds familiar? You don't want to work in a company like that. If you mistakenly did so, start looking for a new job; even if the pay is good, it is not worth the harm it will do to your Emotional Bank Account (Chapter 05).

When you are an interviewee, you tend to look at the company culture too much (use glassdoor for that). Although it is important, even more important is the subculture of the work group that you'll be assigned to, as well as the personality of your direct supervisor. Talk to the people who are going to be your direct co-workers and see if you want to be like them. How do they carry themselves? Are they motivated? Look at their desks, how they dress, etc. Ask them to tell you the truth about their boss and observe how they respond; do they show enthusiasm or hesitation and concern? If possible, offer to take your potential future boss to lunch and watch for signs of self-aggrandizement, entitlement, and narcissistic personality in his or her behavior. Does he talk about himself ALL the time and barely ask questions about you? If your future co-workers seem to be doing well and carrying themselves with dignity, as well as your future boss is a good-natured person, that is great news. Green light. If you find the opposite, employees carrying themselves with a sad body language, while their boss walks around like a superstar, you're much better off passing on that and looking elsewhere for work.

Although you want to prevent taking the wrong job as much as possible, there are great lessons you can learn by working with difficult people, such as asserting yourself, getting antagonists to cooperate with you, defusing competition and jealousy, etc. Sometimes the worst jobs are the best schools. In this case, it is OK to stick around temporarily, but you should move on before it takes too much of a toll on your Emotional Bank Account.

Jobs for leaders: if you are interested in having a 9-to-5 job, embrace your leadership qualities and advertise yourself as such. Look for companies that reward performance. Narrow down your job search exclusively to openings for leadership positions, as a middle manager for example. To help on your quest for the right position, attend leadership programs such as the "Leadership Development Series"

JUMPSTART

from Oklahoma State University and get certified. You can talk about your natural leadership talents but having a certificate will back that claim. Having a 9-to-5 job that allows you to exercise your leadership talents may be an awesome experience. You may find happiness and fulfilment without the stress and the risks that having your own business entails.

If you couldn't find the leadership position that you desire and you desperately need a job, then apply for non-leadership positions as well. In this case, spare yourself from frustrations by <u>accepting in advance</u> that you may never get to be a leader in your new job.

Look at it as a steppingstone and stay there as little time as possible. The longer you stay, the more frustrated you will get and the more afraid to leave you'll become. Of course, If you're lucky, you may be recognized for your leadership abilities and get promoted, but maybe you won't; statistically speaking, if in that company you have one boss for every 10 subordinates, then with no other contributing factors, your chance to be the boss is only 10 percent. Besides, if you do a great job in your non-leadership position, they might just want to keep you in that box. For example, I work as an engineer for Kicker, and I am fully aware that they just don't want me anywhere else but in the R&D (research and development) floor, because I did extremely well for them. I was able to grow financially and become their chief electronics engineer, but they have no interest whatsoever in having me in a higher-level leadership position such as a team manager, for example. To be true to my leadership nature, I have no choice but to leave this job or make my way into a position of leadership—which I am working towards.

To make matters worse, many non-leaders become "the boss" simply because they *have been there long enough.* This often results in an inapt supervisor that may be insecure, overly controlling, and overly stressed, thus making everyone under their management miserable. Inapt supervisors slow down the company's growth because they are not focused on *what's best for everyone*; instead, they're just trying to keep their status and authority, possibly derailing morale.

Even worse, if you're naturally a leader, the inapt supervisor will see you as a threat!

<u>Jobs for non-leaders</u>: People that are happy to follow someone else's lead just need to make sure they don't fall in the comfort-zone trap like many do. Job security is an illusion, my friend. Even the most established companies can be put out of business by a new disruptive business model and/or financial crisis. For this reason, keep sharpening your sword so you never find yourself old with bills to pay, unemployed, and unattractive in this competitive job market. The key is to grow continuously. But how? One way is by creating a *system for growth*, as explained in *How to Fail at Almost Everything and Still Win Big*, by Scott Adams. This system may be something like, "every five years, I will look for a new job or position that requires me to learn new skills and pays me a little more." Now your goal is to execute this system. By doing that, you accumulate knowledge, experience, and stay on the forefront.

If you are happy where you're working at, the good news is that often you don't need to actually work elsewhere to continue growing. You can work in different positions within the same company, thus accumulating new skills and experiences and actively contributing to the company's vision.

In this case, you can ask support from your employer to attend trainings that will grow your skill set and allow yourself to work at different positions. If you work with mixed professionals, you can always learn new things from them. Volunteer for new duties outside your comfort zone.

<u>The best form of job security is to be a desirable professional</u>. After working at different companies, you can always pick your favorite one and re-apply for a position there. Companies that value seniority and have a good holistic culture are usually the best to work at long-term and eventually retire from.

Chapter 20

4.5 pages | 6 minutes

Getting a RAISE

Asking for a raise is a wonderful opportunity to improve your financial compensation, as well as open the eyes of the company management to the qualities of your work and personal character.

- The time to ask for a raise comes when the value you bring well exceeds your salary.
- Before asking for a raise, update your C.V. and LinkedIn profile, as well as search for other jobs.
- Build momentum, and time your request for a raise strategically.

I had been only two years into my job and managed to get a raise of 40%. The key to be successful in your request for a raise is preparation: first, your work-ethic (Chapter 13) must be well established. Second, you need to build *momentum* by creating *as much value as possible* in a time frame preceding your request—six months, for example. If possible, time your raise request to be right after a significant accomplishment, such as the acquisition of a new skill, completion of a project, or the launch of a product that you worked hard on. I timed my request to be right after completing the Kicker KEY amplifier; as soon as great customer reviews started to pour in, I knew it was the perfect time to ask! Your image and attitude also matter a great deal: pay careful attention to your personal care, use good vocabulary, write grammatically correct emails, have a respectful demeanor with others, etc. Make sure to always keep these areas on point. It helps to *look like* you already got that raise (giggles).

Fundamentally, it must make *business sense* to pay you more, which is directly related to the value you bring. To better understand that, think of a time that you needed some sort of work done for you; it could be plumbing, maybe website building, repairing a car, etc. Did you look for "crappy and cheap" or "good and priced fairly?" With that in mind, tell me, what is the worst kind of service? Crappy and expensive. What's the best? Excellent and priced fairly. Between you and your employer, it's not different. You may be an employee, but above that, you are a *service provider*. If your service is crappy, it needs to be cheap, but if your service is GOOD, then it should be priced accordingly! The better your service, the higher you can price it while still maintaining the fairness between quality, quantity, and cost. This ratio NEEDS to be unquestionably right, always.

For the management team to perceive you as a high-value individual, first you must perceive yourself as high value. Are you really bringing more value than you're getting paid for? If the answer is "yes," then it is time to ask for a raise! Think of it as YOU offering THEM the opportunity to continue your employment by adjusting the compensation to be compatible with the value you bring. Also avoid asking for a raise frequently, unless your value has really increased; otherwise, you won't be taken seriously.

By the time you are ready to ask for a raise, you should be equally ready to switch jobs. For this reason, update your C.V. and LinkedIn page; then research other places to work before asking. You might even interview elsewhere and get salary figures from different companies that you could work for. In this way, you'll ask for a raise with much more confidence, knowing what salary amount is fair, and that if they don't match your salary with the value you bring, you can actually work elsewhere where they will recognize your value and pay you better. If your request for a raise isn't granted and your pay is unquestionably less than the value you bring, then it's time for a new job.

JUMPSTART

Okay, let's work on your letter requesting a raise! First, make sure you rely only on positive <u>facts</u> to support your case, completely leaving out feelings, wants, complaints, comparisons, and implicit threats. Keep it short, sound, and sweet—never more than two pages long. Second, please COMPLETELY FORGET the word "raise"! From now on, we will use the word "adjustment" instead. In my letter, the title was "**A**djustment of **F**inancial **C**ompensation" (AFC). This denotes fairness. Asking for a "raise" sounds like you are asking for a **favor**—not beneficial to you! Instead, you're asking for an <u>adjustment</u> to your salary. This means that you're offering to the organization the chance to *meet the value that you have already been bringing*, by adjusting your salary according to the evidence that you will present. In doing so, they get to keep you there longer and happier, which is good for *them* too! Make sense?

Start your letter by showing gratitude to the reader, thanking him or her for the work opportunity you have been given. When the management gets your letter requesting an AFC, they will naturally be defensive. By thanking them first, you are off to a friendly start, and they will be more open to consider your request.

If you are newly hired and this is your first time requesting an AFC, think back to past experiences you have had that help you perform well at your job now; these experiences could be from prior jobs, college, and even hobbies and independent work or study. When I asked for my first AFC, I explained how working on my own projects prior to getting hired have helped me to do my work well on a daily basis at Kicker. For this reason, my AFC was not based on the mere two years on the job, but on a total of twelve years!

Describe with passion how your creativity (Chapter 22) helps you find out-of-the-ordinary solutions to their problems and how that helps them achieve their vision. This is especially helpful if you don't have many years of experience. Often a person with no experience finds new and better ways of doing things because they resort to new, creative methods—there's a lot of value in that. At your work, what processes and tasks can be optimized? Can you find creative solutions to old problems?

Whenever possible, take on a few extra responsibilities, especially the kind that are above your paygrade—without stepping on other people's toes, of course. For example, if you are a junior accountant, can you do some of the work that is expected from a senior accountant? When writing your AFC letter, make sure to emphasize everything *extra* that you did, especially the higher-level work that you took the initiative to learn and execute.

To secure the higher pay you want, from the management team's point of view, your letter needs to answer the question, "What's in it for **me**?" In other words, it needs to demonstrate what benefits THEY would get by paying YOU more. To accomplish that, you need to 1) demonstrate how they *have been* getting a bargain for all the good work you've been doing so far with your current salary, and 2) show how they will *still be* getting a bargain, even when paying you MORE. This will be easy if you do well during your preparation period. With a tone of enthusiasm, elaborate on how you've been a top-performer at their organization. Use bullet points to highlight specific projects with specific dates, especially those that you were able to complete on time or even early. Strongly elaborate on everything "extra"—as described above—that you've done for them, showing your appreciation for having *the means* to do all that great work inside their organization.

Finish your letter with the following steps:

1- Find the highest paying job description/salary that closely matches what you *actually* do.
2- Based on that, ask for the specific amount that is fair for both parties and, optionally, give them the courtesy to know to what noble ends you will use the extra money. For example, are you going to pay for extracurricular activities for your kids with the extra money? If you do, it's worth mentioning.
3- Specifically make the commitment that you will continue to overdeliver.

JUMPSTART

The word "overdeliver" means two things: 1) That the company is getting a great deal in this negotiation and 2) That since you will still be over-delivering even when they pay you more, paying <u>anything less than the value you requested is probably not fair</u>. Thus, you are using their own sense of fairness to grant you higher pay, especially considering that the extra money is for a good cause.

Chapter 21

5.5 pages | 7 minutes

Money Management

Managing your dollars well comes first, making more money comes second. If you manage your money properly, chances are that you will ALWAYS have money, even if you make very little. Unquestionably, this is one of the best and easiest skills to learn - it's a crime that it is not taught at school!

- Limited money teaches you to become good at managing lots of money.
- Not all debt is equal. There is bad debt, stupid debt and good debt.
- Net worth and cash flow work together. Pay attention to both to gauge where you are at; avoid negative net worth with negative cash flow at all costs.
- Watch this complementary video to learn how to budget using a spreadsheet editor.

There are people making minimum wage that manage to save money and people making 6 figure salaries drowning in a pit of debt. We tend to obsess too much about making more money, while overlooking how to best manage the money that we already make. The truth is that if you treat money well, it will always be there for you. Do you make very little money? Great. Take this chance to become an excellent money manager, then once you make more money, you will be incredibly good with it.

JUMPSTART

Making little money forces you to get your priorities straight and resist instant gratification. Take for instance $50.00 USD: it can buy you two uDemy programs, a WordPress website or an app for your business on Fiverr. Or you can buy a few drinks at a bar. To jumpstart your life, focus on spending money on what makes money, and leave out frivolous expenditures—that builds character, my friend.

Cash flow (CF): It is the relationship of how much cash flows IN from job paycheck, side hustles, sales, business profits etc., versus how much cash flows OUT with by paying rent, investing, paying bills, gas, etc. The first cash flow that you need to know is your own. Generally, a positive cash flow means you're building wealth, whereas a negative cash flow means the opposite. Even with a low paying job you can have positive cash flow, because it depends more on the quality of your money management, than the size of your paycheck.

A positive cash flow (good) means that there is more cash flowing IN than flowing OUT. That is ALWAYS your goal. Think of your bank account like a bucket with a drain hole, you want to have more water flowing in than flowing out, thus always having water in the bucket.

Rich or poor, your expenses need to be less than your earnings, period. Your cash flow can be improved just as much by lowering your expenses, as by increasing your earnings. Which one can you do immediately? Probably lowering your expenses. Of course, I'm not advising anyone to live a mediocre life of deprivation, but as a temporary measure to get you off the ground, it may very well be necessary. As you lower your expenses, work on increasing your earnings—read Side Hustle (Chapter 18), Getting a Raise (Chapter 20) and Create Value (Chapter 23).

If you're not making any money, or, if your job pays very little, you need to lessen your housing expenses. If you're living by yourself, consider getting a roommate to split the rent & utilities. Alternatively, you can move back to your parent's house. This can hurt your pride, but it is only temporary until you increase your cash influx, by finding a better job, getting a raise, etc., enough to be able to pay for all your expenses (including housing) and still save part of your income. Read the "The history of Ray" on Chapter 08 for a practical example of using this strategy.

If you're just breaking even and unable to save any money, you're simply spinning your wheels and not getting anywhere—meanwhile, your life is dripping through your fingers. If getting a roomie or moving to your parent's place means that you get to save and invest your money, that is a sacrifice worth making. Remember that this sacrifice ends as soon as you increase your cash influx enough to accommodate your housing expenses and still be able to save.

<u>Savings:</u> As I mention in the Chapter 09, saving is a great habit! Doesn't matter how little you make, you can always save at least "something." Chances are that you can live with 90% of whatever you're making and set aside 10% for a rainy day. If the government were to raise the taxes so it would eat yet another 10% off of your money, you would complain about it, but you would pay it anyway. So why not do that for yourself? Set up an automatic withdrawal to move at least 10% of your income from your checking account to your savings account. Make your goal to save 30% of your income, because 10% is a good starting point but it is not enough. 30% Will get you "there" much faster. I used to save 10%, and as soon as I got a salary raise, I bumped up that quota to 30%. Make *paying yourself* a priority, my friend! If you don't want to bury your money on a 401k that would strike you with a penalty for touching your own cash, I would recommend no penalty certificate deposit accounts to get started, like [this one from Ally](), until you find a better way to save and invest your money.

<u>Debt:</u> There's good debt, stupid debt, and bad debt. Bad debt puts your future and your dreams in jeopardy. Stupid debt is unnecessary debt that only delays your plans but pose little or no risk. Good debt helps to make your dreams come true and even has tax benefits.

Bad Debt is the dream killer—especially high interest credit card debt. In this case, here is what you do: 1- lessen your expenses down to the bare minimum, 2 - pay as much as you can of the bad debt, 3 - save *something* for yourself; if you save $25 bucks every month, at the end of the year you have an emergency fund of $300. If your car battery dies in freezing weather, you can buy it out of this fund, instead of aggravating even more your credit card debt (if you have it, of course). There are credit cards that have <u>0% of interest for the first year</u> and allow you to transfer your existing balance to it. Just google the following words, "credit card no interest balance transfer," and find them. In doing so, your existing credit card debt won't grow any bigger for one entire year, in which you must WORK YOUR BUTT OFF during this "grace period" to pay it off, or at least reduce it greatly—this should be your highest priority goal until you're free from the tentacles of high interest debt.

Stupid Debt is the king of middle-ish class staying stuck. A good example is buying or leasing a new car. Making the payments every month is relatively easy, and it feels great to have a new car; but that car draws on the money that could be used towards more productive things. A car is something that takes money out of your pocket, and therefore it's a **liability**. Stupid debt can turn into bad debt, for example, if you get fired from your job. Don't give in to stupid debt for the sake of instant gratification (Chapter 15). It will only delay you from achieving your true and worthy goals.

Good debt is the dream enabler and maximizer. The general guideline is that you borrow money to buy something that, without requiring your time, makes more money than the payments that you need to make. That's what is called a performing **asset**. Examples:

If you lease a car that costs $400/mo., including wear and tear, insurance, gas, payments, etc., and you get to bring home $700/mo. by UBER driving it, your cash flow is a positive $300. However, that car takes <u>your time</u> to be DRIVEN, otherwise, your cash flow is a negative $400. This time would be better spent creating value, for example. Therefore, the car is NOT a performing asset.

If you buy a house in which the sum of the mortgage, plus tax and insurance is $850/mo., but you rent it out for $1200/mo., your cash flow is a positive $350 requiring little or no time of yours, while building equity in the house itself. That house is a performing asset.

Here is another hypothetical example: imagine that you have a business that nets a profit of $5,000/mo. You carefully do the math and conclude that if you spend $50,000 to expand your operations by buying new equipment and tools, your business will grow to net a profit of $9,000/mo. However, you don't have that kind of money at hand, so you borrow it from the bank to pay in 5 years with an interest rate of 6%. Based on that, your monthly payment for this loan is $967. Therefore, $9,000 - 967 = $8,043. Hence, by responsibly expanding the business operations using good debt, not only that loan is paying for itself, but it is also yielding an extra 61% in profits as your cash flow grew by **$3,043.** Moreover, you get a tax deduction for the depreciation of the new equipment acquired, which means even more money in your pocket! That is EXCELLENT debt, my friend.

See? Not all debt is created equal, there is good debt, and there is bad debt.

Net worth: Is the result of what you own minus what you owe. In other words, it is how much money you would have if you sold everything you have (house, car, furniture, your Nintendo games, etc.) plus all your money, minus everything you owe (mortgage, car payment, etc.).

As long as your cash flow is positive, a negative net worth is not necessarily bad. For example, if you purchase a multi-family home by taking a loan of higher value than the sum of the value of everything you own (including your cash), your net worth will be negative at the time of the purchase.

However, that being a multi-family home, you can rent it out and have multiple tenants paying you rent. The sum of these incoming rent payments should cover for all the property maintenance, tax, mortgage and insurance payments, and still yield a significant profit. This is a good negative net worth and positive cash flow situation. As the mortgage gets paid by your tenants, the equity increases and the debt on this property decreases, and eventually the equity in it will be

JUMPSTART

higher than the amount owed, consequently your net worth will be positive again and you will have lots of equity in this piece of real estate—very good scenario! It's low risk and the negative net worth is only temporary.

Last but not least, **AVOID a scenario of negative net worth with negative cash flow at ALL costs.**

Recommended Watch: [The Company Man (2010)](#)
1h 44min | Drama

Chapter 22

4.5 pages | 6 minutes

Imagination & Creativity

"Be a dreamer and a DOER." Only dreaming gets you nowhere, and only doing things can only get you so far; but when the vision is *combined* with the work, the sky's the limit—except for Elon Musk, of course.

- Imagination is the seed of every human achievement.
- Creativity multiplies the results of your efforts.
- Money problems and lack of experience can be overcome by creativity.
- A Provisional Patent is an inexpensive way to protect your idea(s) for up to one year.

The first complaint I hear from people that are stuck in life, is "I don't have money." We all know that money makes money, but so does creativity and imagination. If you're stuck in life, it's time to think out of the box!

By the end of 2015, I was at the rock bottom. I had invested all my savings painstakingly creating the Audiosigma CarDSP from scratch, betting everything on it—a development cycle done entirely out of my tiny bedroom in Brazil, starting in 2012. This could've worked well, as I successfully created value—as we will see in the next Chapter 23— and therefore, had something real to sell and get paid for.

Unfortunately, that's not how it worked out; I had the misfortune to deal with a crooked company that took my design, manufactured and sold it without paying me a dollar for it. Even worse, their build quality was bad, and they burned the product on the market. Anyhow, my point is, after years of effort I was back at square one! I was disoriented and, to be honest, quite desperate.

After depleting all my savings creating the said CarDSP, which I pretty much *threw it out of the window* by negotiating with the wrong people, I had no choice but to quit being an Entrepreneur and get a "real job."

But HOW? Because I am self-taught, I HAD NOTHING TO SHOW on a C.V., not even a bachelor's degree. Anyone fresh out of the college had better chances to be hired than I would. Imagine this: American dude with bachelor's degree V.S. Brazilian dude with high school education only. Clearly, odds weren't in my favor.

In hopes to remedy this decaying situation, I wrote an 87 pages long resume with all my real-world achievements, abilities, photos and patents. I sent it out to a bunch of companies in Brazil and in the U.S. and had ZERO response—further aggravating my hopelessness and insecurity.

Once I calmed down, I had the idea of making a VIDEO resume instead, short and exciting. I made the video quite accelerated, this way engaging my potential employers to look at what I wanted to show them. As a result, I got not one, but FOUR job offers, the first one being from Kicker—their email came in just three hours after sending out the video! I was dumbfounded. Even though the content of the video was THE SAME as the resume, the result was completely different; presenting that same content in a more creative way made all the difference in the world. In no time, I was on an all-expenses-paid international trip to attend to Kicker's job interview. Thanks to creativity, I was unstuck!

Whenever you resort to creativity to overcome limitations such as money or experience, not only it works, but it often yields much better results. Apple managed to create an affordable computer (the apple II) way back in 1977 with COLOR output, thanks to Steve Wozniak having NO PRIOR EXPERIENCE with video colors. Woz—as they call him—came up with "this little idea" (his words) using a one-dollar chip to generate video colors, and it worked just great. Experienced engineers from IBM just couldn't have imagined that because they were so caught up in their complex engineering practices—they probably would've laughed about it.

The dark side of experience is staying within the comfort zone of how to go about doing something, and consequently, being unable to imagine better, more efficient, perhaps even simpler ways of doing it. As an engineer I see that all the time. I find incredible how "experience" is such a strong requirement to get hired—it bothers me. If you are interested in a position that requires experience and you don't have it, go to the interview and humbly tell the interviewer that although you don't have much experience, you're willing to learn and that you can assure them that your creativity and drive will more than make up for it. Leverage "not knowing" to your advantage, because oftentimes, it is actually a really good thing. The key is to use experience to aid creativity instead of killing it—unfortunately that's not what most people do.

As kids we had no problem imagining ourselves being astronauts, but as we grow up, we tend to lose the habit of *imagining amazing things* and having *crazy ideas*. To the extent that we lose this imaginative habit, we shut down our own possibilities of an extraordinary life. We think that we *outgrow* our childish imagination, when in reality, we're just *censoring ourselves* and becoming skeptical. The key is not to "outgrow" imagination, but rather, to channel it to work in real life with real problems. That's what industrious people do, they see real-world problems and use their imagination to solve them.

Your creativity is more likely to sprout in the area that you have been absorbing the most information. Your brain will work out the magic in the back burner and you don't have direct control over it, but you have 100% control over what information you are feeding your brain to work with. For this reason, choose to read, watch, listen, smell, and taste information that is related to the field in which you desire to become more creative. What did you love to do as a kid? Did

JUMPSTART

you EVER get to work with anything remotely related to it? If you want to have a side-hustle (Chapter 18), do something that the "little you" would be curious and excited about—if the little you approve of it, it's probably a good thing!

If you have an idea that seems great, <u>maybe it IS a great idea</u>. You may think, "Who am I to be the inventor of this idea? Someone else must've done it before me." Well, you'd be surprised how often that is not true. In this case, I suggest you create a Provisional Patent Application (PPA). In short, it's a way of protecting your idea for up to one year, and costs only about $70 dollars. With a PPA, you actually get a <u>patent number</u> and can approach well established companies to share your idea(s)—and hopefully get paid royalties for them. I do NOT recommend you getting an expensive "traditional" patent on anything before first doing a PPA and really exploring whether the idea makes sense in the market—if it indeed has a future in the real-world, or not. The thing is, traditional non-provisional patents can cost over ten thousand dollars just to file for, then you will have to pay maintenance fees on it, and even pay lawyers to enforce it should it get challenged. It is tough! That is fine if you're already making money off of your idea, but that can break your legs if you're just starting.

Go to YouTube and search for "What is a Provisional Patent," learn about it, then execute your own PPA. If you're really serious about it, I'd recommend reading the book "Sell Your Ideas With or Without a Patent" from Stephen M. Key.

Equally important to pursuing your ideas and dreams, is to NOT GIVE A CRAP about anyone who says that your dreams are "too grandiose" or anything of this sort. I*t is your birthright to dream*, you can and should do it. The difference between a dreamer and a successful person, is that the dreamer just didn't do anything about it, whereas the successful person pursued these dreams vigorously. Allow yourself to dream, unafraid and unashamed, then set the goals (Chapter 08) and take action (chapter 10) to make them come true.

Lastly, we ALL need a reality check and good advice from time to time. To get such good advice, <u>share your dreams only with those who</u>

<u>meet or exceed your own capacity of achievement</u>, especially those who have "made it." Don't ever share your glorious future plans with people that don't meet this criterion, as they will most likely tell you that your dreams are impossible. **If you hear such a thing, be sure that this is a reflection of, not yours, but their own inability to attain that which you proposed to yourself.**

I'd like to quote what Jay Samit, author of the amazing book "Disrupt you," said in an interview. I'm paraphrasing, but it goes like this:

"If you do something that others are doing, you're going to have competition and you gotta be really, really good; but if you do something that no one else is doing, by definition, you're the best in the world." — Think about that!

Chapter 23

4.5 pages | 6 minutes

Create Value

You may be thinking, "I need money to make money." It is true in many cases, but not always. What if you're starting from scratch, with zero money? How do you create money "out of thin air"? You don't. First, you create value; then you transform that value into money.

- Ideas, creations, and skills have value.
- Value and money are different things; you generate money by selling the value that you first created.
- Whatever you're creating, unless you take it to the finishing line, it has little or no value.

Imagine a demolition wrecking ball. The big heavy ball that hangs from the top has no power in a standstill state, but when it swings, it has the power to take down houses and buildings. Think of <u>value as the weight</u> of that wrecking ball and of <u>sale as the swing</u> of it. The more value you create, the more potential power there is; the more you SELL the value you created, the more you convert that potential power into buying power, a.k.a. money. What is more powerful, a huge wrecking ball that never moves, or a small wrecking ball that is at full swing? The latter, of course! That's why it is important to create value, but it is equally (or more!) important to sell the heck out of it! Examples of value include inventions, training, consulting, coaching, book writing, YouTube videos, logo design, blogging, etc.

JK Rowling, the author of *Harry Potter* was living off welfare, skipping meals to feed her baby daughter, and even borrowing money from friends to pay her rent. She turned her life around by creating value: every day she would go to the nearest cafe to write. It took her five years to complete the first *Harry Potter* book, but once completed, she had all that *potential value* in her hands. Thankfully, she persisted in SELLING this value because not one, but TWELVE publishing companies refused to publish the first *Harry Potter* book. She continued to seek a publisher until finally one publisher in the U.K. gave it a shot.

As the book started to grow in popularity and finally got to the U.S., much to her surprise, American publishing companies started a bidding war to publish her book. One publishing company paid her the sum of $105,000.00 in advance, which allowed her to work full-time as a writer, continuing her saga from book two to book seven. She officially became a full-time *value creator!* By book number three, her books were already the top three NY Times best sellers. Her money problems were OVER. She created VALUE from scratch. She did not have to have money to make her first money; she just consolidated the power of Creativity (Chapter 22) with the power of Habit (Chapter 09), and in time, the result of her efforts came to fruition.

In the process of creating value, you become more valuable yourself—this is called *intrinsic value*. For example, in the process of creating a product, you can learn many new valuable skills. If the product sells, then you have successfully generated money from the value you created. If the product fails to sell, you still retain the value of your learning. Suppose that *Harry Potter* had never been published; as Rowling's writing skills were much improved by simply writing the book, it would've been easier for her to be hired and well paid as a professional writer. In other words, her perseverance would've been worth it anyway.

In fact, this is how I got hired, without a college degree, as an electrical engineer at Kicker. I literally went from my bedroom in Brazil to their headquarters in the U.S. as a result of my two previous entrepreneurial adventures with Acousticlass and Audiosigma—both companies that failed. I had no money, but lots of intrinsic value.

JUMPSTART

When you become a valuable person yourself, others will want to hang out with you, associate with you, hire you and, of course, gladly pay you.

A financially rich person with poor intrinsic value is quite a sad thing to see; no one likes a rich and ignorant person. I don't mean "ignorant" in the sense of education—but in the form of wisdom and experience. My grandpa Toufic had no schooling whatsoever, but he became a wise and experienced man. As a poor immigrant from Lebanon, he arrived in Brazil not even knowing how to speak Portuguese—he literally walked off the boat with a dictionary in his hands. He started off by selling inexpensive merchandise on the streets and fought his way up to become a real estate expert.

He passed away, but the building with his initials "T.C.E" will continue to stand tall in downtown São Paulo *. To everyone who knew him, what always stood out were his words of wisdom accompanied by his humble and calm ways. When people with high intrinsic value become rich, they are able to stay rich; if they lose their fortune, they're able to rebuild it because they have the necessary tools *inside* of them. Don't just strive for money, strive for intrinsic value! And strive for money too, of course! (giggles).

There are two ways to sell the value that you create: the first and riskier method is to create something that you believe will sell and then find your paying customers later. The second and more guaranteed method is to find your paying customers first and THEN create the value for them.

Usually, people that are more of the creative kind, approach selling their value with the first method. The issue with it is that you may spend a great amount of time, effort, and money creating something to later find out that there aren't many people—or NO ONE—out there to pay for what you believe is valuable. I know that from experience, as I failed miserably with my first patent of the "StudioAMP" in 2008. The advantage of this method is that it gives you more freedom to create and make your own vision come true.

For example, for fiction books (like *Harry Potter*), usually you just need to write them the best that you can and then hope that people will love and purchase them. With this method, there is little market research, but you can truly create the market for something new. Like the iPod for example—people didn't know they wanted to buy an iPod until they saw one!

Normally, the people that are more business oriented, approach selling their value with the second method. The great advantage of this method is that you are almost guaranteed to have the monetary returns for your investments. Artists and inventors can also use this method; it's just not as *appealing to the heart,* but it may very well be *more filling for the pockets*—LOL! As soon as you find the paying customers, you basically have "money waiting to happen!" All you have to do is create the value that they are <u>already looking for</u>. For example, imagine that you sit down with a few CEOs and ask them what their biggest pains are in the management of their groups. Then, based on their responses, you create a method to facilitate their group management, freeing up the time of the CEOs as well as increasing harmony and productivity of their employees. How valuable would that be for them? Would they pay you for that? Absolutely! And that is consulting, my friend.

Now, let's take it down a notch and think about how you can apply that in your life if you are the employee in the workforce. You can simply sit down with your supervisor and ask, "What is the skill that, if I learn and execute well, will help us achieve our mission?" In other words, you're asking, "How can I bring the *most value* to our team?" In this case, your paying customer is the company that you already work for. Once you learn and effectively apply this new skill at work—bringing measurable results—, you automatically earn a raise in salary; then all you need to do is to claim it (Chapter 20).

Whatever is it that you're doing to create value—whether it is learning a skill, creating a project or business, writing a book, etc.—, keep in mind that it has little or NO VALUE unless you finish it. Many people, including myself, have the habit of not finishing what they start. A book half written is worth nothing, a perfectly good car without tires cannot be driven, an incomplete invention cannot turn into a selling product, etc. I personally tend to lose interest in whatever I am working when it is time to wrap up and take care of the final details and corrections—because that final stage is SO BORING! Nonetheless, I force myself to finish it, then check and recheck. Had I not grabbed this damaging habit by the neck, I'd still be a failing like crazy. **You start by being creative, but you finish by being methodical!**

* My grandpa's building:
R. Santa Luzia, 48 - Liberdade,
São Paulo - SP, 04233-080, Brazil.

Recommended Watch: <u>The story of Joy Mangano (2015)</u>
2h 04min | Biography, Drama

Chapter 24

6.5 pages | 8 minutes

Fundamentals of Products and Services

Having a business may or may not fit your personality. Some people crave having their own business and are happier that way, others prefer to be an employee and forget about work as soon as they leave the office. There's no right or wrong, what's best is what makes you happy, my friend!

If you think you have what it takes to create a business and provide jobs, then you probably should. The fact is, everyone needs work, no exception; but not everyone is willing to go through the risks and difficulties involved in having their own business—and creating jobs as a result. Understand that when you grind, when you persist and succeed in creating your business, you're helping many more people than just yourself.

- If you can't compete, innovate.
- Stating your mission properly helps create loyal customers
- Initial price of your product or service is largely limited by your reputation
- For physical products, logistics, manufacturing and pricing need to be well thought out.
- Products and services don't need to be perfect, but need to fit the market very well.

Innovate: Usually it is quite difficult—but not impossible—to outperform your competition in the beginning stages. For this reason, you might want to focus on innovating, more than trying to compete with well established businesses with a similar offering of product(s) or service(s).

Keep in mind that innovating and inventing are different things. You don't need to invent something completely new in order to innovate. For example, Piggly Wiggly was the first ever self-service grocery store! Before them, you were not allowed to go get the groceries from the shelves yourself, you had no choice but to ask the salesclerk to do it for you. They didn't invent grocery shopping, but certainly they innovated it and prevailed.

To effectively innovate, all you need to do is to improve upon an existing product, service or model of business, or differentiate yourself enough to appeal to a new and untapped audience. Actually, it's arguably better to innovate than to invent. A good example of innovation is the self-wringing mop from Joy Mangano (refer to the movie recommendation of the prior chapter); everyone already knew what a mop is, Joy simply made it better.

If you improve upon something that is already known and accepted, your chances of succeeding are excellent, whereas if you invent something completely new, you'll need to *create the market* for it. It is a lot of work, and it's not guaranteed to pay off. However, if your invention solves a major problem or a hurdle, you may take off like a rocket, simply because you have created a brand-new solution that works better than anything else for a long existing problem. Read "Blue Ocean Strategy," by W. Chan Kim and Renee Mauborgne for more specifics and important information on this topic.

Lastly, if you're innovating an existing and well accepted product or service, and especially if you are inventing something brand new, much of your success will rely on the quality and strength of your marketing. What I mean is that, no matter how great the value you bring, it's worth nothing if it remains in the dark. If you're not sure that you can do a good marketing job, I recommend that you either team up with someone that can, or improve your marketing skills.

Velocity of sales: When you create a physical product, make sure you can keep up with the demand in case it ramps up. A high demand is a *good problem* to have, but it IS a problem, nonetheless. My first product, the LiveClass, offered excellent value, plenty of innovation, but it was very difficult to manufacture; it required hundreds of components and it was a very slow process to build one. As a result, I could not supply the demand after its initial exposition and that caused the product to die off quickly. Lesson learned. Of course, you don't need to worry about it when it comes to digital products and services such as phone apps, online courses, digital books, etc. You can simply replicate it as many times as you wish and always supply the demand without worry.

If you're into making a physical product, make sure that the assembly process, storage and logistics can be as hand off as possible. If you're really clever about it, you can create an extra-ordinary product using just ordinary materials and easy manufacturing. It all comes down to your design and how much effort you put into making it as simple as possible to be manufactured. Pay special attention to constraints such as cash flow, storage and manufacturing (consider outsourcing that part, as well).

Minimum Viable Product (MVP): First you need to TEST the market and see if your product idea works by making the smallest investment of time and money. For that, create your MVP. It must contain the most important features and not much else. It must do its job and doesn't need to be fancy. The faster you get the feedback from the market, the better. With that feedback you will improve upon it and, over time, add more bells & whistles. The goal here is to verify if your product indeed fits well a market. A perfect product that doesn't fit the market is sure to fail, whereas an imperfect and even rudimentary product that fits the market like a glove, still succeeds and allows you to make new and better versions of it by listening to the feedback of your customers.

Niche vs. Mass market: If you're venturing with physical product(s) you may be better off creating something for a specific market niche. The coolest thing about it is that you get to know your customer, establish a relationship with them, and grow your business organically. In this case, your selling price can be a little higher, so you actually have a good profit margin, given that your quantities won't be large—at least not at first. A good rule of thumb is that your product must retail for at least four times your build cost, but preferably more. If you design a product that costs $15 and you sell it for $99, then that is a healthy 6x ratio. In the beginning of your operations, you need to focus on delivering excellent value, making very cost-effective products to attract people willing to give it a shot for the first time. However, the more you build your reputation, the more accepting of a higher price tag your customers will be. It's a growth process! Examples of niche products: tools and equipment for recording studios, laboratories, etc.

If you came up with a physical product that is a mass market item, something that can be sold at Walmart, Amazon, Best Buy, etc., and that the average person would want to buy, there's a very high likelihood that the moment you start selling it, pretty soon fake copies coming from China will sprout like mushrooms. If your operation is rather small and you're unable to take a big chunk of the market, chances are that the Chinese knock offs will dominate the sales and you won't even be remembered. For this reason, you're probably better off licensing your product to a large and well established company that will have a strong market presence from the get go. Examples of mass market products: smart light bulbs, inexpensive Bluetooth speakers, household tools, etc.

For digital products, you don't have to worry about the Chinese flooding the market and pushing you out of it. Therefore, both specific market niches and larger mass markets are great. For small niches, you are allowed to price your product higher and make better profits. Examples of niche digital products: management softwares for a specific type of business, training programs for a particular industry field, etc. Examples of mass market digital products: e-books, online training programs, dating apps, etc.

Today I am working on three different products: a fancy headphone amplifier for a small niche of recording studios—I am choosing to venture with that one, a smart light bulb that has a few innovations—I am in the process of licensing it to a big company—, and finally, this book that although it is for a mass market, it's something easy to replicate and distribute.

<u>Know the size of your audience:</u> Whatever product, service or solution you create, it must serve a large enough number of people. Even niche markets must be large enough to accommodate a foreseeable growth.

<u>Have a clear proposition:</u> Be specific to what it does, how it does it, and for whom it does it. If you're opening a restaurant, don't try to please both vegans and steak eaters. If you're a stake eater yourself, you want to serve steak. If you're vegan, you want to serve vegan food.

<u>Branding:</u> To create something that stands the test of time, it's important that you state your mission. For example, once I resume the operations of my company Acousticlass Audio, our motto will be "making you sound amazing." Why? Because it states our MISSION. Truly, I want anyone that purchases an Acousticlass Audio product, to have a big smile on their face when they play music with it.

Successful brands successfully state their mission, for example, Apple's motto is "think different." Kicker's motto is "Livin' Loud." And so it goes. When you get to the consumer's heart and successfully make a statement that resonates with them, you will be in business for a very long time, my friend. By the way, my motto "Making you sound amazing" is probably too long, I might have to think more about it (giggles).

<u>Offer "great value."</u> There is a reason why the Walmart branded products are called "Great Value." They're not there to offer passion, they're there to offer VALUE—and it works. Until you win the hearts of your customers through effective branding, you have to appeal to their brains instead. Conquer their brains first, then later conquer their hearts. You can conquer their brains by offering more quantity, quality and features for less money when compared the competition. Sort of <u>like Hyundai very aggressively did</u> to establish themselves by comparing their value proposition with other brands; they would

compare themselves to Mercedes and BMW in terms of features and performance, and yet, their price was lower. Their message simply was "we're the best bang for your buck, and here is why." For the skeptical folks, they backed it all up with extended warranties. Feel free to compare yourself to other competitors, always offering an advantage and something reassuring, like "satisfaction guaranteed or your money back." It's not pretty, but it does work. And of course, it must be indeed true, or you'll be shooting yourself on the foot.

Customer care: Better than being in business for the new customers, is to be in business for the returning customers. The more you establish a relationship with them, the more you understand them, the better. You can create a following that will swear by you and your products. Refer to the chapters about Work Ethic (13) and Criticism (12) for a bigger picture.

In general, make a point to improve the relationship with your customer in every single communication with them, for whatever reason this communication occurs. When I sold a bunch of LiveClass P.A. systems in Brazil, I've had quite a few of them break and need repair or replacement. Obviously, when a customer contacts you because the expensive thing they bought from you broke, they're not in the best mood. I would hear their complaint without any resistance whatsoever, sincerely apologize for the inconvenience, and assure them that in three working days the unit would be repaired at no cost. Right there and then, I could sense the relief that my customer felt. They would ship it back to me, and as soon as I received the package, I would send them an email confirming the receipt. Then, I would stop everything I was doing and get straight to work on fixing their broken unit, and either the very same day or the next day I would ship it right back to them and send yet another email with the tracking number. Beyond that, I made sure to thoroughly clean it and pack it as if it were new. Actually, because the housing was painted with an automotive glossy metallic gray, I went as far as waxing to give it a sparkling shine. Every single time, they got their unit pristine condition, looking good, smelling good, and faster than they imagined. I over-delivered in the repair. The people that spread the best and most passionate words about the LiveClass and my business, were these very customers that were disappointed in the first place.

    <u>To have or not to have your own business:</u> Last but not least, how do you know if having your business is really for you? It's simple. You just feel like there is no job in the world that will ever make you as fulfilled and happy as having your biz. It's a dream, it's an itch you have to scratch, it's a personal necessity. You would prefer making 75k / year doing your thing, rather than 250k / year working for someone else. Even making a modest income with your business makes you feel like a million bucks. If this resonates strongly with you, then you have no choice.

Chapter 25

4 pages | 5 minutes

DISRUPT your approach!

Success is a product of keenly leveraging your skills and choosing the approach best suited for each phase of your life. Even if your approach worked well in the past, it doesn't mean that it will continue to work for your future — ESPECIALLY if you envision a future that is very different from your present and past circumstances.

- Leveraging your existing skills can be better than learning new ones.
- Your approach must be a function of your environment and your skills.
- Your skills and approach may become obsolete, but your work ethic never does.

Today there is an epidemic of people trying to get better at whatever they do—better singer, better engineer, better kitchen chef, better hairdresser, etc. While I strongly encourage you to constantly progress and get better at what you do, that is not the whole picture.

The truth is, no matter how good you are at something, even if you're incredibly exceptional and off the charts, poorly leveraging your skill(s) will not yield good returns! A great fisherman fishing on a lake with low fish count will catch fewer fish than a not-so-great fisherman fishing on a lake with plenty of fish. Sometimes, the key is not to get better at what you do or learn a new skill, but rather, leverage your existing skills better. Find a way to do what you love that gives you the best return for your efforts. In the case of the fisherman, he is better off choosing to fish on a lake with more fish than getting even better at fishing. How can that apply to you? What would be the equivalent of a *lake with more fish* to you? Think about it.

Your approach is what comes before choosing *what lake to fish*; it is the form in which you choose to go about life. It's "the big picture." People usually hate to change their approach because their identity is too heavily attached to it, and it is a lot of work to reinvent oneself. Usually, people cling to what worked in the past and try very hard to *make it work* for their future, but it isn't always possible, especially because everything around you WILL change over time. Michael Bloomberg initially chose to approach his career as an electrical engineer. He is worth $62.1 BILLION dollars today. Do you think he could accumulate this fortune by working as an employee at Samsung? Not in a million years. Instead, Bloomberg changed his approach, not once but several times, always leveraging his *good-with-numbers* skills differently each time and adapting to his new circumstances.

Imagine that two brothers from Oklahoma, John and Jeff, are both graduates with majors in math. Jeff has always been a bit better skilled than John, being able to solve more complex math problems with ease. Upon graduation, both Jeff and John became math teachers, and for 10 years they worked together in their home state; they were making a living, having just enough to pay the bills. When asked the question, "What do you do for a living?" both would answer, "I am a math teacher." When you hear them saying, "I am a math teacher," it means that they chose to approach life as an educator by using their math skills. Unfortunately, teachers get paid less than they deserve, especially in Oklahoma. Although John was not as bright as Jeff, he couldn't help having a lingering degree of frustration and dissatisfaction, so John decided to take action. The first thing he did was to move to New York, where he instantly got paid a better salary than Jeff. Along with that, John started to tutor students struggling through college on the side. Most of these students were willing to pay good money for John's tutoring in mathematics. As a result, by

JUMPSTART

teaching in NY and tutoring students on the side, John was making more than twice as much money as Jeff was. Jeff was intrigued and inspired by John, but he did not want to move out of Oklahoma. Still, Jeff did start to tutor students struggling through college on the side, just like John was doing. Turns out that the students in Oklahoma couldn't pay much for Jeff's help, and for this reason, Jeff had to lower the price of his private lessons to a modest amount. Financially, John was many steps ahead of Jeff. The difference was that in NY, not only was the base salary higher, but there were many more students that could pay well for math tutoring than there were in Oklahoma. The fact that Jeff was a bit more skilled and talented than John practically didn't matter. In other words, John was fishing out of a lake with plenty of fish whereas Jeff was fishing out of a lake with fewer fish; John was leveraging his skills better!

    John was doing well, paying all his bills, living with comfort and a few luxuries, but he wanted more. John recognized the limits of his approach, which is to say, of being *an educator that teaches math*. He envisioned for himself a completely different lifestyle in which he would be retired by the age of 45 with passive income and a net worth of at least a few million dollars. As much as John enjoyed being a teacher, he recognized that his approach would not get him there, that he had pretty much *maxed out* how much money he could make as a school teacher.

    Initially with the humble goal of getting better returns on his own savings, John started to take an interest in investing. He went to www.meetup.com and started to attend investor meetings, networking with real estate investors, stock investors, angel investors, etc. In this process, John discovered that these wealthy investors could certainly use his help, and they could pay John much more for his time than students could! Because he is *good with numbers*, he could help them to better analyze investment deals, maximizing their profits and minimizing their risks. What a profitable use of his existing math skills! With his modest savings, John bought a beautiful suit and shiny shoes, which he utilized to attend these investor meetings and meet potential new clients. John also invested the time and the effort to make a great LinkedIn page, a personal website, and business cards. He knew that a professional image is important to get the credibility he deserves, and thus, get the best returns for his skills and efforts. Leverage, leverage, leverage!

From the beginning, John made investments himself in order to effectively learn what works best and what doesn't. As John learned more about investing, he created a series of professional YouTube video tutorials and even published his own eBook on Amazon. John never hesitated to work hard on building his reputation as an *authority*, because he knew that the more knowledgeable he became, the more investors would pay for his time as a consultant. It took him a few long years, but John effectively became an asset for very wealthy people, and therefore, got paid large sums of money for his consulting. Moreover, John's credibility became so well known that he was able to get private financing from multiple investors, therefore using OPM (other people's money) to expand as an investor himself! At this point, John had effectively disrupted his approach, transitioning from an educator to a consultant and investor. John's profits grew exponentially, eventually reaching his goal of retiring wealthy and under 45. John dedicated the rest of his life to creating an army of teachers to educate those in poor countries that couldn't afford to pay for their own education. John helped himself so well that he chose to spend the rest of his life helping others; his retirement was only the beginning of his life's work. What a worthy goal!

Takeaway: Jeff was more skilled, but John became more successful. Had John become even better at his math skills and continued to be a teacher in Oklahoma, he would have benefited little or nothing from it; he would have been stuck, like Jeff. Instead, John first better leveraged his existing math skills by teaching in a wealthier area. As a result of having access to wealthy investors in his new environment, John disrupted his approach by retiring from being a school teacher to become a consultant and investor, which paid him much better dividends. John took action and backed it all up with a

JUMPSTART

solid work ethic, always going the extra mile by putting in the time, work, and effort required.

Chapter 26

11.5 pages | 20 minutes

Finding your ROMANTIC partner!

"May you both be different in your strengths and weaknesses, but similar in your way of life and future aspirations." This phrase dawned on me one day, while driving.

- The more compatible you and your partner are, the more you can focus on building the relationship and a future together—instead of "finding balance."
- You should never give up your dreams to be in a relationship.
- Discover your and your partner's love languages and improve your communication.
- Don't ever let "being nice" take priority over being HONEST.
- Cultivate a fulfilling sex life together, especially to reap the long-term benefits.
- Live by the best of each other, let leadership be fluid and based on merit.
- Love someone for their human-being qualities, not just for their human-doing qualities.
- Understanding your attachment style is key to forming a new and healthy relationship.

It's incredibly easy to *identify* ourselves, as well as *advertise* ourselves, not for who we are, but for what we do. I can say that I **am** an engineer, but in reality, I just "do" engineering. However, what we DO sometimes gives us *clues* of who we are—but not always. For instance, engineers tend to be quite logical and pragmatic, whereas artists may be more sensitive and idealistic. It's not uncommon that what someone does, doesn't quite reveal who they are—or may even be in contradiction—, so we can't rely much on that. Do you want to be in love with a person, or with what that person does? What we do changes, who we are rarely changes. Therefore, when in search of a partner, it's always best to focus on who we/they are, rather than whatever it is that we do. When you meet someone for the first time, it's natural to talk about the things that you guys do, but as much as possible, try to deepen the conversation to find out if you guys are on the same page about your core values.

When you love your partner for who she is, even when she's not **doing** what you like or approve of, you can still work things out because you love her as human-*being,* rather than exclusively as a human-*doing.* Imagine that your partner suffered brain damage and lost ALL her skills, talents, experiences, etc., while at the same time, fully retaining her personality, that being her character, sense of humor, ability to love, temper, the way she talks, walks and laughs, etc. Would you still love what's left of her? Because that's who she IS, separated from everything else that she does. That's the base of unconditional love, meaning that specific conditions don't need to be met in order to, well, love. Otherwise, the moment that she stops doing whatever makes you like her (such as shared activities), the "love" disappears—because you "love" her only as a human-*doing*. You can't marry someone based on that. Likewise, you want someone that loves you for who you are, not exclusively for what you do. But yes, what a person *does* matters a lot, as we'll see.

Provided that the both of you have this discernment, there are very practical considerations that need attention; people are free to choose what they do and how to live their lives, and there's only so much you can compromise in this aspect. In my naivité, I sincerely believed that all it takes for two people that love and respect each other to have a successful relationship, is *persistence and work.* This is only half of the truth; the other half is the *compatibility* between you and your partner, both on a daily basis, and into the future.

To be compatible on a daily basis, your way-of-life should be somewhat similar, whereas your strengths and weaknesses are best when different and complementary—in general, of course.

The way-of-life is how an individual conducts him or herself on a daily basis and what makes them happy; that includes: how early you wake up, level of personal energy, degree of introversion and extroversion, type of humor, exercise, diet, lifestyle, faith, political view, time management, level of hygiene, how you prioritize work, family and friends, etc. Different personalities require different forms of nurturing. There are people who look for a quiet and simple existence, and others that want to be active and grow continuously. If what floats your boat floats your partner's boat as well, you're in good shape! In this case, similarities are great!

Imagine that Jane is loving, truthful, honest, compassionate and intelligent—those are her *character traits*. Jane's way of life is slow paced, frugal, traditional, organized and content—that's the way she naturally lives her life. John is loving, truthful, honest, empathetic and intelligent. John's way of life is fast paced, lavish, unconventional, messy, and dissatisfied with the status quo. As you can see, John and Jane have most character traits in common. However, their way-of-life is diametrically opposed, and as much as Jane & John want to be together, most likely they won't succeed in the long run. It's a strange concept that two people can have similar character traits, and yet, not be a great match—but it happens.

Strengths and weaknesses are, for the most part, skills and emotional response. Have you heard that business advice, "Never hire your clone"? It's applicable here too. A creative person that is full of ideas for businesses can really benefit from a more structured partner that reads the small print on contracts and is well organized. One person may be good at making money, while the other is great at keeping money—together they get to make it and manage it well. Two hot headed people drive each other crazy, whereas a hot headed and a cool headed one are usually a better match. When one person is good at what another struggles with and vice-versa, both win and are better together. In this case, differences are generally good!

To be compatible walking into the future hand in hand, your dreams and aspirations need to line up well with each other. Simply put, if one person wants to be a millionaire and the other wants to be a missionary, meeting in the middle just won't work—as they are headed in completely different directions. In this case, *"finding balance" is not the answer*, because a good relationship should help each of you achieve your dreams—rather than existing at their expense.

This is a more flexible matter if you and / or your partner don't have a fixed idea of what you want out of life; but nonetheless, make sure you and your partner are on the same page—revisit Chapter 1 and discuss what success means to each of you. Have fun playing with that idea for a while! Then, create a shared vision for the future and figure out how you guys can cooperate with each other to achieve it—this is guaranteed to bring you guys close together. This vision may include location to live, type and size of the house, number of kids and pets, lifestyle, health and wealth, countries you would like to visit, general "bucket list" items, etc. Based on that, set your goals (chapter 08) together and, as much as possible, define the *roles* that each of you will play in the attainment of your combined vision. The key is to *pursue together* this shared vision, whether you'll accomplish it or not is a different story, the benefit is more on the pursuit itself than in the realization per se.

The less compatibility you have, the more you will have to adjust and compromise to be together, and it can get to a point that you may *lose your edge*, maybe even lose your priorities and sense of identity if you're not careful. There's obviously no limit to how compatible you guys can be, but the opposite is not true—just like you can't make a square fit in a circle! If you find yourself compromising in areas of your life that you consider top priority, you might just be with the wrong partner. The more compatibility you have, the more you will direct your energies to actually BUILDING the relationship AND a future together, rather than "adjusting"—that's what I call an *energizing relationship*.

For the aspects in which your way-of-life differs too much, there has to be *understanding* rather than blaming. The issue becomes worse when the way-of-life of each person differs in so many aspects that, instead of integrating, they resort to living mostly parallel lives— a "you do you" sort of thing. "Yeah, go do your diet and run a marathon, I'll wait for you here while I eat my cheerios and watch TV." This actually makes me cringe.

It's fine—and healthy—to operate independently in some areas, however, when there's too much of that going on, you can't help but to grow emotionally distant from each other. On the contrary, shared activities are a great way to grow the connection between you guys. The truth is that you want enough *overlap* to have a real connection, but not a complete eclipse in which you lose your sense of identity. As we'll see next, cultivating these shared aspects of life and consequently the emotional connection between you and your partner, can have a wonderful positive impact in the sex life of you guys.

How important is sex? Well, it depends. How important is it for you? Sex drive is different for each person and in relationship to age as well. You're best matched with a person who consider sex just as important as you do, whether that is a little or a lot—no judgment. Simply ask, "how important is sex for you?," and, if the importance is a 9 out of 10 for one and just a 5 out of 10 for another, you've got a problem. I just want to loudly say that, for me, it's VERY important because I want a partner, not a roommate. In this case, you really need to cultivate a good sex life—otherwise, being unfulfilled in this area leads either to infidelity or sexual frustration.

Sexual attraction is not fixed and won't last forever, but years (hopefully decades!) down the road, you want to celebrate how good you had it with your partner. We all know too well the short-term benefits of it, but even more important, is the long-term bond that sex creates: when you see a cute old couple walking together holding hands, chances are that they had a great sex life, my friend. Who knows, maybe they STILL do! (giggles).

Men and women are quite different when it comes to sexual attraction and emotional connection. In simple terms, men usually need to start off with a strong sexual attraction, as it is unlikely that they will develop it as a result of an emotional bond. On the contrary, women do build sexual attraction out of emotional connection.

If you're a man and met someone that *fits the bill,* but you're not sexually attracted to her, it's probably best that you don't even try—for your own sake, and especially for her who will feel unwanted. You may bond emotionally with this person and yet never develop the sexual attraction, as a consequence, end up seeing her just as a friend—this situation would be crushing for her. However, the same is not true for women, as often they do become sexually attracted to someone that they weren't initially, as a result of a meaningful and loving relationship; in other words, women actually can start a relationship with someone that they are not particularly attracted to, if their partner possess the qualities they're looking for. Likewise, women often lose their sexual attraction for someone that they were initially attracted to, if the relationship fails to fill her emotional needs.

In sum: Men should not initiate a romantic relationship with someone they're not attracted to; by nurturing the heart of your lady, it is likely that she will be motivated to nurture the sexual life of you guys. Women should not initiate a romantic relationship with someone that is unable to nurture them emotionally; while in a relationship, by nurturing the sexual aspects of it, your guy is likely to become more emotionally invested as well.

Openly talk about your *turn-ons* and *turn-offs*. This ranges from the way you dress, your habits, to the things you say and the way you like to be touched, etc. Make a pact to cultivate the turn-ons and to **not slack off** with the turn-offs. If you guys share the same toilet, be especially mindful of that. If you have not a burning flame but a spark for someone amazing, triple down on cultivating it, otherwise that spark may be gone before you know it and that would be a sad ending for you guys. I hope you find a compatible partner and that you guys can't keep your hands off each other!

Your partner will be your strongest "influencer"—For good or bad, she has the power to influence your goals, finances, diet, health, and even your relationship with your parents, family, friends, co-workers, etc. That's a BIG deal, my friend. Therefore, ask yourself: is my partner mostly a positive or negative influence on me? And how about the quality of MY influence on her?

Provided that you influence each other mostly in a positive way—otherwise it's a toxic relationship that needs to end—, when your partner has a negative influence on you, work on being tough minded and keeping the course, doing your best to not let yourself be swayed by this negative influence. Also, let them know about it, explain why, and ask to stop it. When your partner has a positive influence on you, just let yourself be influenced without creating resistance, and praise / thank her for being this positive influence—she will feel amazing! In other words, <u>be stubborn for the negative influences, but vulnerable to the positive influences</u>. Please understand that, when you don't make yourself vulnerable to your partner's positive influence, not only you don't progress, but most likely you'll make your partner unmotivated, which can cause her to retrograde as well—not cool!

With that in mind, <u>make the decision to progress together</u>; that means striving to live by the best of each other. For example, imagine that Kayla is great at keeping the house well organized, but she has a tendency to eat unhealthy food. On the other hand, Gabriel is great at eating healthy, but he is quite messy around the house. From the moment that Kayla & Gabriel start living together, they will begin influencing one another. Should they slip into influencing each other negatively, both will end up messy and eating junk food—and resenting each other for that. Should they decide to influence each other positively, both will become well organized and with healthy eating habits—and happy about each other's influence. Simple! Sit down and talk about these aspects and choose who's going to lead in each area, with the goal of mutual gain and progress—that of course requires you to put your pride away and cherish everything your partner is good at, as well as humbly admitting what you suck at and letting go of it.

So far, we've talked about making a pact to live by the best of each other, openly talking about sex, setting goals together, etc. Well, all that requires good communication. Practice, practice, practice it. Different people have different communication styles—this is especially true for introverts vs. extroverts—, and therefore, the first thing that needs to happen, is finding how each of you best communicate. This is a great area to compromise and find balance. If you are an introvert, get out of your comfort zone and practice talking face to face with your partner. If you tend to talk way too much, practice restraint and give leeway for your partner to have his or her turn as well.

Discover each other's love languages; for example, Mario's primary love language is "acts of service," such as filling up Angela's car, just to spare her the trouble of having to go to the gas station herself. However, Angela's primary love language is "words of affirmation," and therefore she needs to actually *hear* from Mario loving words. Unless Angela *learns* that when Mario tops up her car he actually means "I love you," she may feel unloved. Having learned that from each other, now Mario can make an effort to actually say the words, just as well as Angela may practice acts of service for Mario to feel loved too. In fact, just having this comprehension already makes them both feel more loved, as they will recognize the love coming from each other in different ways. For example, before Angela knew that Mario's first love language is acts of service, she just appreciated conveniently having her car always filled with gas; now, *knowing* that this is Mario's form of expressing love, she actually feels loved when she gets in the car and sees that it's been topped up. Learning each other's love languages is a game changer, my friend! The five love languages are: Words of affirmation, physical touch, acts of service, receiving gifts and quality time.

If you're successful, you'll reach a deep level of intimacy, where you can share with your partner even the most embarrassing things. Discuss your needs, the things that you are willing to change, your non-negotiables, and stay always on the side of the truth—even if that means "not being nice." During conflict resolution, put the relationship first and yourself second; listen not to find fault and strike back, but to understand your partner and find resolution together.

Speaking of "needs," find out what YOU need and what your PARTNER needs from the relationship, and see if you can indeed nurture each other. Sometimes one gets their needs met while the other doesn't. "You can't move forward with someone if you can't or are unwilling to fulfil their needs and desires, it's pointless" — Stephen Labossiere.

By the way, "being nice" is concerning. Yes, we should care about the feelings of others, but "nice" can easily become dishonest. Simply not telling the whole truth about something because you may be afraid of how the other person will feel or react about it, is already dishonest. It's not hard to be dishonest—not only with others but with yourself as well—for being "nice." For example, if you stay in a relationship that doesn't fulfil you and you keep acting *nice* by pretending that everything is well, you're being completely dishonest with yourself and your partner. In sum, HONEST FIRST, nice later. Commit to being completely honest when communicating with your partner.

Being honest doesn't mean being super blunt and not caring about how your partner feels. You can and should find the kindest words, as well as the appropriate moment to have difficult conversations. Like a good friend of mine said, "the term 'brutally honest' raises a flag for me"—and I agree. Once you say something, you cannot take it back. For this reason, if there's something critical and potentially devastating to be talked about, I encourage you to take your time to process it, instead of just saying things on an impulse. Question yourself first, before questioning your partner. Different people have different views of the world, and for this reason, be mindful of when you're about to have a difficult conversation based on your *assumptions* of what is true, good and correct. Your truth may not be the whole truth. I'd say that for most critical conversations, one week is usually enough time to process it, and for less critical ones, one day should be fine. Everyone is different, but remember that the more you drag something, the more your partner suffers. Process it, but don't procrastinate it.

Obviously, here we are focused on "finding the right one." Quite frankly, I believe that the popular idea of "having fun with the wrong ones until you find the right one" is overrated. If you have a heart, each time that you have to bounce back from the pain of a failed relationship, at least temporarily, you're compromised in your ability to govern your life—breakups are painful, and divorces are devastating. For this reason, why not get it right sooner than later? Turns out that, as I've heard, "choosing the right person is <u>more important than everything combined</u> that you can do to make your marriage succeed," therefore, choosing wrong and then trying to "make it work" later, is a failed strategy.

With that in mind, I ask you to give up the idea of trying to *win-over* someone. The key is to *be yourself* right off the bat on the first date—if you want something real and lasting, you don't have a choice. Use the beginning of a relationship to truly discover each other, understanding that if you have to walk away from it, it's best to do so while you're not so invested in it—especially emotionally. Talk about your way-of-life and aspirations, if you guys are compatible, taking a "no filter" approach won't drive you apart, but rather, bring you guys closer together to an amazing start!

Even when two wonderful and really compatible people meet, the beginning of a relationship can be a challenge, particularly the first dates and texting back and forth. For this reason, it's very important to understand your *attachment style.*

There are essentially three types: secure (healthy), anxious and avoidant. We pretty much have all of these to different degrees, but we're usually most influenced by one style or two. The good news is that IF the relationship consolidates in a healthy way, the tendency is that both individuals grow their *secure* style—essentially healing.

In large, we don't choose our attachment style. If you grew up with fear of abandonment because your parents didn't make you feel secure enough or even neglected you, then you're likely to have an anxious attachment style. If your parents were emotionally disconnected and dismissive, not meeting your emotional need for connection as a child, or worse, if they behaved in a violent and traumatizing way, you're likely to have an avoidant attachment style. Beyond that, traumatizing and abusive relationships later in life may exacerbate (or perhaps even create) unhealthy attachment styles in a person.

People with an anxious attachment style usually worry that their partner will leave and it takes them a while to feel at ease and relax, knowing that their partner is not going to just disappear for no good reason. Because of that, they're usually very tense in the beginning of a relationship until it solidifies enough for them to feel some sense of security. Unfortunately, often that becomes a self-fulfilling prophecy as they tend to behave in a way that is off-putting to the other person, for example, by being "clingy" or "over texting." Does it mean that this person is a bad match? No. It means that this person needs to understand why he (or she) feels that way and make a conscious effort to not be controlled by this fear.

On the other end of the spectrum, people with avoidant attachment style may be craving to be loved, to meet that person that will rock their world and touch them in every level, but they have their guard up and seem almost impossible to get to. They believe that their needs can't or won't be met, and it also may become a self-fulfilling prophecy. Again, the solution is the same: understanding oneself and not letting that pattern repeat. In this case, the key is building trust and letting the guard down as the other person proves his (or her) good nature and intentions.

The good news is that, provided that two well intended and compatible people come together, attachment styles may be just a

JUMPSTART

temporary challenge—unlike incompatibility of core values, for example. Knowing that, try to understand your own and your partner's attachment style and get past that.

Finally, although *compatibility* is a real thing, character hardly ever changes, whereas compatibility issues can be tolerated and improved. If your partner is truly a good human being, I'm optimistic you can work many of the compatibility issues out, after all, there's no such thing as a perfect match. In terms of priority, character comes first, compatibility second, and attachment style third.

Chapter 27

4 pages | 5 minutes

The Plan TODAY

How happy are you about your past? Well, good or bad, it was shaped by the quality of the days you've lived, one by one. Your FUTURE will also be shaped by the quality of the days that you are about to live, one by one. If a successful life is simply the accumulation of more good than bad days, then how can we make today good and tomorrow a little better? It's simple! To the BEST of your abilities, commit to always maintain, frequently progress, and not regress on the following aspects of your life:

- **Health**: Physical, Mental, Emotional and Spiritual.
- **Finances**: Your credit, balance, debt, etc.
- **Social**: Significant other, friends, family, business partners, etc.
- **Big picture goals**: The pillars of your future life.

If you can't advance all of the above on the same day, that's perfectly fine. If you only so much commit to <u>always support</u> and advance them occasionally, you're looking pretty good already. *Supporting* simply means caring and maintaining them—it is the opposite of neglect. *Advancing* means actively doing something to improve it. For example, if you're on a mission to lose weight, supporting it means stepping on the scale and being conscious about where you stand; advancing means hopping on the treadmill and breaking a sweat.

JUMPSTART

This is what a typical day of mine that supports and advances all four aspects looks like: I work first thing in the morning on my side-hustle, this way, advancing my big picture goals. Then I go to my 9-to-5 job and I am fully invested in the tasks at hand, which guarantees the continuity of my salary which I still need. At lunch break, I check my bank account balance and credit score, thereby supporting my finances. After work, I go to the gym, advancing my health. Back home, I work again on my side-hustle, this way, I continue to advance my goals for the future. At any point I like to call or message a friend and, by doing that, I am supporting my social life.

This plan works simply because you are consciously seeking to take care of the most meaningful aspects of your life every single day. Most problems, whether that be financial, social or health related, come from <u>cumulative neglect</u>. By executing this simple plan, you effectively eliminate the possibility of neglect and make progress inevitable.

We all need to walk before we run, so, for the moment, just focus on getting yourself to consistently support these four areas of your life, pretty much never "dropping the ball" in any of them. Trust yourself that, once this plan becomes a habit, you will desire to advance each time more. You will succeed by taking doable steps ahead, and only you know how big of a step you can take at a time. In this process, you will evolve from "stuff falling apart" to "having your stuff together," and then become increasingly successful. As you see the benefits of your actions compounding, you will become more enthusiastic and further increase the rate of your forward progress.

Success is being a little better off tomorrow than you are today, because of something you did TODAY. Success is being MUCH better off in 5 years than today, because you *have been* doing a little better every day. Success is a moving target that keeps us thriving, growing, and most importantly, finding joy in the process.

We all have infinite versions of ourselves in the future; we pick which version we will become by our actions today. For example, if you are neglectful, you're choosing a pretty unhappy version of yourself in the future. If you're diligent in supporting the most meaningful aspects of your life, you're choosing a healthy and happy, but perhaps not extraordinary version of yourself. But if you're both diligent in supporting AND advancing these meaningful aspects of your life, then you're choosing the HERO version of yourself! With that understanding, picture this "hero" version of yourself 5 years from now: what poor personality traits did you overcome and what good aspects of your personality did you expand on? What does your health and finances look like? What new things you've learned to do and what are your accomplishments?

With that in mind, let the hero-you that exists 5 years from now coordinate your thoughts and ACTIONS today. If in 5 years you imagine yourself happily married, you won't have an argument with your partner; instead, you might be inspired to go out on a romantic date with her or him. If you imagine yourself in good physical shape, you won't eat that donut, instead, you'll go hit the gym or walk around the block. If you imagine yourself with plenty of savings, you won't spend your money buying stuff that you don't need. And so it goes. It's SIMPLE. <u>Think 5 years ahead to coordinate your actions TODAY</u>.

Sure, there will be moments of setbacks, tears, rage, anger, or even hopelessness. Sometimes bad stuff just happens! Deal with these bad times the best you can, remaining calm as much as possible. The bad times today don't define your future. <u>How you handle the bad times, does</u>. These moments serve a purpose—they often correct your course and exercise your emotional muscles, such as being patient and having a good attitude in spite of difficult circumstances. Always remember to see the benefit of the problems that arise—most problems carry opportunities within them. Many people became successful after getting fired! If you're hammering a nail into wood and it starts to tilt sideways, you want to straighten it up as soon as possible, so you can continue to hammer it DOWN and not sideways. That's what these "setbacks" are for. There's an upside to almost every bad situation. In those cases, ask, "What are these hard times telling me to do?."

JUMPSTART

Bad days do happen, even to the happiest and most successful people—sometimes, shit just hits the fan! On days like this, there are three things you can do: <u>1- Surrender</u>; a bad day is a bad day, don't try to make it pretty. Fully embrace "the suck" and just do the best you can during that day. If you've got some terrible news, don't try to deny it, instead process it in full—cry if you have to. <u>2- Set up for a better next day</u>; If at all possible, whatever you can do on that "bad day" to have a better next day, do it. For example, working late on something dreadful so you don't have to deal with it the next day. <u>3- Do at least one thing right to feel good about</u>; it could be the laundry, cleaning the dishes, replying to an overdue email, or taking the trash out—whatever that is. Just do ONE thing that you can feel a bit good about—even if it is a small, seemingly meaningless thing.

TODAY, will you make a promise? Don't promise that you will advance every item on the list *no matter what* because there are things out of your control that can prevent you from keeping this promise. Instead, promise that YOU WILL NOT STOP YOURSELF from having an excellent day in which you support and advance these four most important aspects of your life.

Print out the text below and read it every morning for a minimum of 21 days; let it be the first thing that you see when you first wake-up. You will notice how your ACTIONS will change because you have consciously put your brain on the right track before anyone else—or the TV news—had the chance to derail your mind. As a result, your days will get better and better.

Lastly, keep in mind that although one day alone will not change your entire life, it will absolutely change how you will feel at the end of the day. And it is the accumulation of these better days that make a happy and successful life.

HAVE A GREAT DAY, MY FRIEND!

Two copies of affirmations will follow on the next pages, so you can detach one off the book and stick it to the wall, while the other remains on the book.

JUST FOR TODAY

1 - Just for today, I will think and act like the person I would like to become; starting with what I choose to eat, watch and listen, as well as how I talk to people, utilize my time, efforts and money.

2 - Just for today, I will plan ahead what I expect to do in the morning, afternoon, evening and night. By doing that, I will eliminate stress and confusion.

3 - Just for today, my actions will support and advance my big picture goals, health, finances and social life; today none of my actions will go against these four most important aspects of my life.

4 - Just for today, I will be my best friend. I will talk myself into doing the things that are good for me long-term and out of the things that may feel good at the moment, but that can delay or hinder my goals. I will encourage and trust myself to delay gratification and to do what is best.

5 - Just for today, I will take my chances, be daring, and keep in mind that failing is to quit early or to not even try; I will be strong and trust my abilities, and if my attempt fails, I will try again.

6 - Just for today, I will not sell myself short; instead of saying "I can't," I'll ask "how can I?" and proceed to the best of my abilities to do that which initially I would not even try doing.

7 - Just for today, I will not let small things or negative people rob me of the vitality that I need to execute my plans and achieve my goals. I'll take full responsibility for my feelings because nothing and no one but myself can directly change the way I feel for better or worse. Today I choose to feel good.

8 - Just for today, I will remember all the reasons why I do what I am doing, especially in the face of difficulties. I will not recognize failure; I will be resilient because my reasons are noble and worthwhile.

9 - Just for today, I'll be well on time and keep my commitments, both to myself and others.

10 - "Just for today, I will act courteously, be liberal with praise, criticise not at all, nor find fault with anything and not try to regulate or improve anyone."*

11 - "Just for today, I will try to live through this day only, not to tackle my whole life problem at once. I can do things for twelve hours that would appall me if I had to keep them up for a lifetime."*

12 - "Just for today, I will be unafraid; especially I will not be afraid to be happy, to enjoy what is beautiful, to love and to believe that those I love, love me."*

*Items with the asterisk were quoted from the book *Dale Carnegie: How to Stop Worrying and Start Living*.

Fernando Eid Pires

JUMPSTART

JUST FOR TODAY

1 - Just for today, I will think and act like the person I would like to become; starting with what I choose to eat, watch and listen, as well as how I talk to people, utilize my time, efforts and money.

2 - Just for today, I will plan ahead what I expect to do in the morning, afternoon, evening and night. By doing that, I will eliminate stress and confusion.

3 - Just for today, my actions will support and advance my big picture goals, health, finances and social life; today none of my actions will go against these four most important aspects of my life.

4 - Just for today, I will be my best friend. I will talk myself into doing the things that are good for me long-term and out of the things that may feel good at the moment, but that can delay or hinder my goals. I will encourage and trust myself to delay gratification and to do what is best.

5 - Just for today, I will take my chances, be daring, and keep in mind that failing is to quit early or to not even try; I will be strong and trust my abilities, and if my attempt fails, I will try again.

6 - Just for today, I will not sell myself short; instead of saying "I can't," I'll ask "how can I?" and proceed to the best of my abilities to do that which initially I would not even try doing.

7 - Just for today, I will not let small things or negative people rob me of the vitality that I need to execute my plans and achieve my goals. I'll take full responsibility for my feelings because nothing and no one but myself can directly change the way I feel for better or worse. Today I choose to feel good.

8 - Just for today, I will remember all the reasons why I do what I am doing, especially in the face of difficulties. I will not recognize failure; I will be resilient because my reasons are noble and worthwhile.

9 - Just for today, I'll be well on time and keep my commitments, both to myself and others.

10 - "Just for today, I will act courteously, be liberal with praise, criticise not at all, nor find fault with anything and not try to regulate or improve anyone."*

11 - "Just for today, I will try to live through this day only, not to tackle my whole life problem at once. I can do things for twelve hours that would appall me if I had to keep them up for a lifetime."*

12 - "Just for today, I will be unafraid; especially I will not be afraid to be happy, to enjoy what is beautiful, to love and to believe that those I love, love me."*

*Items with the asterisk were quoted from the book *Dale Carnegie: How to Stop Worrying and Start Living*.

Fernando Eid Pires

JUMPSTART

THE PITFALLS

OF SOCIETY

My heart is heavy with the sense of urgency and necessity that prompted me to write the next three chapters—I wish I could simply pretend all is well and ignore these themes, but I feel a sense of obligation to talk about these delicate and controversial subjects.

JUMPSTART

PITFALL 1

4 pages | 5 minutes

Societal Auto-immune Disease

It is clear that we've been more divided than ever, and in large, we've been acting as if a whole HALF of the population are our enemy. If over 98% of the population are good people (and they are), we cannot behave as if 50% of them were "bad"—that is absolutely insane!

- **MOST PEOPLE ARE GOOD** regardless of their political view, act like it.
- **MOST PEOPLE ARE GOOD** regardless of their sexual orientation, act like it.
- **MOST PEOPLE ARE GOOD** regardless of their color, act like it.
- **MOST PEOPLE ARE GOOD** regardless of their religion, act like it.
- **MOST PEOPLE ARE GOOD** regardless of their wealth and status, act like it.
- **MOST PEOPLE ARE GOOD** regardless of their (fill the blank), act like it.

When someone votes for the presidential candidate that you vehemently hate, that doesn't make that person bad OR your enemy, and you shouldn't treat him or her as such. Just remember that, even if their decision is completely "wrong"—from your point of view, which may also be wrong—, that person probably made that very decision out of the goodness of their heart, thinking that it was the better choice, or in the political context that we currently live in, "the lesser of the two evils."

We all have our differences of opinion, in fact, we've had these differences for the longest time—but it didn't break us apart the way it's been breaking us today. Opposing political parties exist since the beginning of politics; people have had different skin colors, eye shapes and culture since the beginning of humanity; social gaps and inequality of wealth and status have existed since the beginning of any sort of economic system, etc. There's nothing new. What's new, is how intensely we're rejecting and judging each other over these matters. Truly most people are good and deserve to be treated as such, as the vast majority of us are capable of acts of kindness, compassion, and just want to be happy—we share the same goals!

Our differences enrich our culture, disrupt our way of thinking, and quite often bust us out of our little world. That's the reason why everyone of us has a different story to tell—ranging from the white gay fashion designer Giorgio Armani all the way to the black fastest running man Usain Bolt. How can we not love that? The amount of variety between us is staggering! If I could lessen the differences between us, I wouldn't dare touch it, but if I could cast a spell that would make us *appreciate* our differences, damn right I would!

I've found this on Facebook and would like to share: *if you catch 100 red fire ants, as well as 100 large black ants and put them in a jar, at first, nothing will happen. However, if you violently shake the jar and dump them back on the ground, the ants will fight until they eventually kill each other. The thing is, the red ants think the black ants are the enemy and vice versa, when in reality, the real enemy is the person who shook the jar. This is exactly what's happening in society today: liberal vs. conservative, Black vs. White, pro-mask vs. anti-mask, vax vs. anti-vax, rich vs poor, man vs woman, cop vs citizen, healthy vs sick, young vs elderly, science vs fear, etc.*

The real question we need to be asking ourselves is, who's shaking the jar and why? No matter who is shaking the jar, do not give away your power. Stay strong in hope, with supportive love for one another. Fear creates closed minded survival tactics. You have the choice to rise above it all. Stay strong in spirit, honor and respect your brothers and sisters. Freedom awaits.

It's well known that stress and a toxic environment can trigger autoimmune diseases on a human body; because it makes the immune system go out of whack, becoming belligerent and attacking even what is healthy and normal. That's exactly what is happening to our society today. By repeatedly pressing upon and aggravating these themes of skin color, political view, sexual orientation, religion preference, etc., we're creating a *societal auto-immune disease*. We're attacking our differences, instead of being respectful, appreciative and curious about them. We're attacking and destroying our own healthy fabric as a society. Just like you can't judge someone based on the color of their skin, it is just as insane to judge a person by who they voted for, for example. It's time to calm down, regroup and reunite. We've been *induced* to act like this by the political landscape and the media, including social media and YouTube algorithms. Let's just not let that get to us anymore. Turn off your TV, ignore the YouTube suggestions, ignore your Facebook feed. They're feeding us hate.

A war has been waged against us, aimed to destroy our natural tendency to be good to each other, to stick together, and have each other's back. You can't fight fire with fire—it only burns more. The only way out is to simply not give them what they want, to simply show them that what they're doing is not working anymore and no longer will ever work. Go be friends with someone with the opposing political view and don't talk about politics. Invite friends of different backgrounds, religions and races over for dinner and talk about everything else but these differences. Start acting like these things are not even something to be talked about, because what really matters is a person's <u>character and intentions</u>. That's how you fight this war, you put out fire with water, not with more fire. Our societal auto-immune disease will only get better by lessening the environmental stress and toxicity.

> "It's sad, so sad
> It's a sad, sad situation
> And it's getting more and more absurd
> It's sad, so sad
> Why can't we talk it over?
> Oh, it seems to me
> That sorry seems to be the hardest word"
> — Elton John

If you are a good conservative person, you are my friend.
If you are a good liberal person, you are my friend.
If you are a good gay person, you are my friend.
If you are a good straight person, you are my friend.
If you are a good bisexual person, you are my friend.
If you are a good black person, you are my friend.
If you are a good yellow person, you are my friend.
If you are a good white person, you are my friend.
If you're a good brown person, you are my friend.
If you are a good Christian person, you are my friend.
If you are a good Muslim person, you are my friend.
If you are a good Atheist person, you are my friend.
If you are a good Buddhist person, you are my friend.
If you are a good rich person, you are my friend.
If you are a good poor person, you are my friend.
If you are a good person that wears a mask, you are my friend.
If you are a good person that refuses to wear a mask, you are my friend.
If you are a good **ANYTHING** person, you are my friend.

If you have a good heart, I already love you. I am already willing to protect you. Even if we are completely different, and even if we disagree on most things.

JUMPSTART

PITFALL 2

7 pages | 10 minutes

Pornography and Human Trafficking

A note for female readers: there's a high chance that your partner, or future partner, may struggle or will struggle with pornography. If you're using online dating, it's almost certain that you are talking to men that watch porn on a regular basis. It's important that you read this chapter.

A note for all readers: I am by no means trying to impose some sort of morale or make anyone feel bad with this chapter. If you feel offended by the content of this chapter, I apologize to you in advance, I respect you and your decisions. Also, I want to remark that although I definitely have a problem with the porn industry, I have nothing against the porn actors, in fact, I wish I could protect them from being scammed and exploited.

In 2020, more than FOUR BILLION hours of porn were watched on one website alone. It's a 97 BILLION dollar industry that generates more traffic on the internet than Netflix, Amazon and Twitter combined. Yes, we need to talk about it!

- Porn often leads to debilitating erectile dysfunction, and jeopardizes your ability to begin and maintain relationships—including marriage.
- It is used like drugs, it harms like drugs, and it's easier to obtain than alcohol.

- Long term, porn changes your brain on a physical level, potentially leading to ADHD, depression, anxiety, inability to focus on work, manage expectations and gratifications.
- Porn desensitizes you to real-life sex by raising your arousal threshold too high.
- Kids begin watching porn at 10 years old.
- Porn finances human trafficking, kidnapping and slavery of people and children.
- Visit www.fightthenewdrug.org

Porn addiction may start out of curiosity, or to fill an emotional need. Emotional needs could be loneliness, anxiety, depression, or to temporarily relieve an emotional pain; it's not uncommon that people would go on a porn binge after a breakup or getting fired. The truth is that the triggers for any drug, porn and alcohol are almost always the same. However, porn is so easily accessible that a small amount of normal curiosity may lead someone to addiction. An average person may wonder what cocaine feels like, but just the trouble of getting it makes that person give up, as the curiosity exists but not to a degree high enough to go through the trouble of sourcing this expensive drug from potentially dangerous people. However, that same tiny curiosity is just enough for someone to type the url of a porn website.

You may simply be alone in your room and, almost innocently, decide to *just check it out*. The vast majority of people won't watch porn only once and then completely forget about it; they will remember it, and be tempted to watch it again—and again, and again... The reason being is that, through your mirror neurons, porn does an incredible job stimulating the rewards center in your brain, releasing a rush of dopamine and oxytocin that is just about perfect for a lonely person in a state of depression, boredomness, stress or anxiety. As this rewards center is wired to keep us coming back to it, you can easily get addicted to pornography, especially if you don't know the incredibly harmful side effects that it causes long-term—such as erectile dysfunction and changes in your brain—, and, the brutally cruel human trafficking industry it finances. By the way, thanks to the Coronavirus pandemic, porn usage has increased over 50%! Pimps and traffickers are probably sitting back and laughing—my heart cries for humanity right now.

Because pornography is still something that people avoid talking about, there are a millions upon millions of people watching it on a regular basis, setting themselves up for failure in their relationships or future relationships. The ball doesn't stop with you, however. Porn also finances the human trafficking and exploitation industry, as we'll see later; but right now, let's focus on you.

There are two major issues with porn that make it even more destructive on a large scale than chemical drugs. The first, as we've discussed, is how easily accessible it is and the fact that no one talks about it. It's very easy to hide a porn addiction, as you won't physically look like an addict. The second is the fact that porn is the only drug that *you can manufacture and get high by yourself alone*. What I mean is that you can only get high on heroin by injecting it, once you no longer have heroin around, you just can't get high anymore—as your body won't *produce* it. However, with porn, you don't necessarily need to watch it again to get high. You can literally *replay* it in your mind, and that's pretty much the same as actually watching it. Truly quitting porn means to stop replaying and fantasizing about it in your mind too, otherwise you'll be activating the same circuits in your brain, and therefore, reinforcing and nurturing those neurological pathways that keep you addicted to it—unless you do that, it will be very difficult to "reset to factory settings."

So, what are the consequences of watching porn? The first is Erectile Dysfunction (ED), and the second, is the disruption of your healthy and natural sexuality—which as a consequence, damages your ability to create and maintain healthy sexual relationships. There is no shortage of men under the age of 30 suffering from ED with perfectly healthy bodies. It makes me so upset to hear the radio blasting ads of "men's clinics" promising a quick fix for ED. I'm sure that there are serious professionals with the best intentions out there, but I'm also sure that there are a multitude of scammers trying to take advantage of these healthy young individuals that struggle with porn.

ED is just half of the problem; porn not only hijacks one's ability to function in bed, but it also changes what sex means. Sex is not just rubbing body parts and a rush of feel-good hormones; it's also trust, connection, vulnerability, communication, and intimacy. All of which are left out in most pornography. In real life these are not mutually exclusive, and what makes it **awesome** is that one day you and your partner may be truly in a romantic act, and another day, you guys may be enjoying more the physical aspects of it—and every nuance in between. That's real life, with a real person that you love, respect and are attracted to; but in porn, it's always just about rubbing body parts, each time closer and in higher resolution. Watch enough of it, and your mind may literally split these elements of intimacy and physicality so far apart that it may become hard to reconcile them. You may feel that if you make romantic love with your partner, you're not having "real sex," and that's a problem. Don't get me wrong, I'm not judging; I'm just saying that you may be in the perfect loving relationship, with a wonderful partner, and still miss "porn sex" to the point that it will either make you frustrated, or, urge you to cheat—does that align with your goals and your definition of success?

Maybe you're young, perhaps in your 20s and not planning to get married anytime soon, but these small changes that you can make now, may be the difference between having a happy marriage in the future or not. What you do in your 20s usually does change the outcome of your life in your 30s, 40s and later, and this is no exception. I'm not suggesting that you only picture "boring sex" in your mind, far from it. I'm suggesting you don't imagine "porn sex" all the time. The goal is to be healthy and ready for a great relationship, and in fact, I admire the couples that allow themselves to fully express and explore their sexuality, unafraid and unashamed of each other within four walls.

If you are in a stable relationship and porn has a hold of you, the best you can do is to open up to your partner. Perhaps, have her read this chapter. Even better, go to www.fightthenewdrug.org and, together, watch their videos. Trust me, a good partner will not judge you for it, and she will support your recovery. This journey may actually create even more trust between you and your partner; whereas you'd be creating a ticking bomb by brushing this issue under the rug. This may first come as a shock and rock the boat, but if someone loves and cares for you, that someone won't *dump* you over this. Would you dump your partner for it? No, right? Same thing.

Porn increases your *arousal threshold* to levels that are hard to obtain and maintain in real life. If you don't watch porn, just seeing your partner take her shirt off may already get you going, whereas a porn addict may go to a strip club and barely get an erection. Porn makes you *desensitized* to sex, and as a consequence, your partner will have a hard time fulfilling your sexual needs—and that, my friend, is not fun for her. In other words, porn is likely to make you sexually frustrated because having "normal sex" is not enough to stimulate you like porn does. Not only that's a problem for your happiness (and your partner's as well) for obvious reasons, but the other issue is that this frustration with sex and the desire to fulfil that need makes you *vulnerable* to scams and even other women that have zero interest in your happiness and wellbeing. Porn won't serve you, whether you're a single young guy trying to make a living, or an older and married millionaire. The effects of Porn may put everything that you've built at a loss, or even prevent you from building an amazing life and marriage in the first place. What you want is the ability to create and maintain sexual fulfilment with your romantic partner, and when the opportunity to cheat arises, be able to turn it down without being tormented by it.

Imaging studies of the brain showed that watching porn causes changes that are connected to ADHD, depression, anxiety, inability to resist Instant Gratification (Chapter 15), and more. People relate having much better FOCUS, energy to work and happiness after quitting porn. In fact, after one to two years of no longer watching it, the shrunk areas of the brain actually grew back and were physically recovered. Now that you're fully aware that porn can put your happiness and future in jeopardy, let's see how bad porn actually is to humanity, shall we?

There's no such thing as the "porn industry," the "prostitution industry," or the "human trafficking industry"—all in separate compartments. They're all the **same** industry. Simply by watching porn on the internet, you're generating revenue for their website, which finances this whole thing. Yes, when you're innocently watching a porn video, thinking that there's no harm to it, you're financing modern-day slavery. Here are some facts about Human Trafficking for you:

- An estimated 4.8 million victims are exploited for sex, trapped in modern-day slavery; half of which are children, and many of which will never get to return home.
- Porn is used to train children that are sex slaves to perform for paying customers. They are punished if they don't live up to the expected "performance."
- When you watch porn, you don't know whether you're watching someone who's getting paid to perform, or someone who is being kept as a slave. You simply cannot tell. If you don't believe me, watch the history of Elizabeth Smart, an American woman that was kidnapped at the age of 14 and kept as a sex slave—TED talk, Wikipedia.
- Even paid porn actors are coerced in doing things that they don't want to do. They are tricked with "last minute" changes and additions that if they don't comply, they get burned in the industry and won't ever be able to work again. Imagine a girl at the risk of becoming homeless because she's not doing "XYZ"—it happens all the time.
- Many porn actors become addicted to drugs and alcohol to be able to perform.

Beyond that, kids are beginning to watch porn at the age of just 10 years old; the greatest issue is that they're getting their *sex education*

JUMPSTART

from it. How is that going to ever work with trust, vulnerability, intimacy, emotional connection, etc.? It won't! Porn is setting up abusive and non-intimate relationships for the future. Can you imagine how much higher the divorce rate will be with this sort of "education"? According to the statistics, children of divorced couples have been shown to have lower grades at school, to be 20% less physically healthy, 50% more likely to develop health problems, 300% more likely to need psychological help, and twice as likely to attempt suicide. How's that for the future of the nation?

So, there you go. Porn not only screws up your relationships, messes up your brain and gives you erectile dysfunction, but it is also destroying our future and financing an industry that is kidnapping, enslaving, sexually abusing and killing children. Are you going to keep watching porn?

To quit watching porn, the first thing is to commit to a time frame that you'll be without it. Start with just one week, then a month, then a few months, then finally an entire year. To accomplish that, you may need some form of accountability. This could be a trusted friend that you can call to talk you out of it whenever you feel the urge to watch it. Another form of accountability is making a *promise*. If you do believe in a higher power (name your God here), you can make that commitment in prayer or meditation. If you don't believe in a higher power, you can promise to your *future self* or *higher self* that you will not watch porn for X amount of time, or *else*... Regardless of any "woo-woo" stuff, one thing is certain: Your self confidence and self regard will be much improved by taking control of this urge, instead of letting the urge control you.

Another very helpful habit is to default to exercise whenever you feel the desire to watch porn. If you went to check your email and suddenly found yourself wanting to open another tab on the browser and visit a porn website, just go take a walk! If you do, listen to an audiobook or podcast with a completely unrelated subject, this way, your focus will change and will be much easier for you to forget about watching it.

PITFALL 3

11 pages | 20 minutes

Unhealthy Financial System

A candid opening note: this chapter is for everyone who would like to see a healthier and fair financial system—regardless of your political point of view. It's all about us doing OUR homework to make things better.

Capitalism is as good as the **morale** and the education of the people participating in it—plain and simple. It's not good or evil, it's what you make of it. Problems such as wealth inequality, monopolies and poverty are NOT caused by the system per se, but by ordinary people making uninformed decisions, and in large, by individuals and businesses that are exploiting the financial system for personal gain without creating any value.

- By choosing where you spend your dollars, you keep monopolies in check.
- If you can afford, don't buy the cheapest stuff, especially food products. This way, you help keep wages up and more ethically correct business practices.
- Try to spend more on local / family business, rather than chain store counterparts.
- It's not a zero-sum game when you create value. Invest, but don't exploit trading.
- Manage your money properly and teach someone how to manage their money properly.

- Pay someone to fix your TV, instead of just throwing it away and buying a new one.
- Embrace the concepts of Sharing Economy and Earth Value—if your generation doesn't need to think about it, the next one will.

The issues that we're currently having—and further aggravating—in our capitalist financial system, have much to do with the wild business and consuming practices occurring every day. Just like in the wild, people can default to "kill or be killed" business and consuming practices that are very detrimental to the economy and our wellbeing—think of the Black Friday fights, or worse, of the people that will buy all the meat from the supermarket shelf, leaving nothing for the next person in line at times of extreme weather or other forms of threat. I want to remark that it's not a matter of "how much capitalism," but rather, "what form of capitalism" instead—that being *ethical* vs. *wild*. Is too much Wild capitalism a problem? Absolutely. Is too much Ethical capitalism a problem? Absolutely not.

When we don't have enough morale, government regulations and restrictions must come in place to avoid disaster. For example, on a road where drivers are skilled and committed to driving well, you may have no speed limit, and yet, have a very small number of accidents. On the other hand, should the drivers be poorly skilled, abusive or neglectful with their driving practices, the speed limit may be severely reduced, and yet, and a lot of accidents will still occur. Basically, this is how I see capitalism; when the participants are good, we need little to no regulation, the freer the market, the better. However, when the business and consuming practices are questionable, you need more regulation to avoid disaster—unfortunately.

The issue is that we can never be sure about the *intention* of those imposing or lifting these regulations—and taxations, as well. What it means is that when WE fail to uphold a good standard, we become vulnerable to crooks making their way into powerful positions of the government, by using a lousy populist speech and pretending to play

Robin Hood—falsely promising to resolve the issues that WE created in the first place, promising to save us from ourselves like a good parent would. Unfortunately, this type of demagogy has been getting more and more traction, hence the sense of obligation I had to write this undesirable chapter.

The quality of a capitalist economy (a.k.a. "Free Market") is directly proportional to the morale of the **sum of everyone** that is participating in it—it's *all inclusive*. The quality of a government-imposed economy (a.k.a "centralized command economy") is directly proportional to the morale solely of those **few individuals** with governing *power*—pay attention to the word "power." Unfortunately, because we're not yet so spiritually elevated and we are morally flawed creatures, it's undeniable that "power" corrupts MANY people. Therefore, if the quality of the economy is defined exclusively by those *in power*, then there's a much higher chance that this economy will be of poor quality—because many of them are sure to be corrupt.

For this reason, even with all its problems, the capitalist economy of a free country is still less vulnerable to the corruption of those in power, than a government-imposed economy—commonly employed in communist countries. If we improve the morale of our business and consuming practices, if we become more aware about the fact that *how we choose to make and spend* our dollars directly affects everyone around us, the economy improves and the problems of wealth inequality, monopoly and poverty that stand out like sore thumbs are lessened to the degree that we evolve. Unless we are governed by actual Angels from Heaven, capitalism will always be the better alternative. We are the cause of the financial issues in our capitalist society, and the change starts with you, my friend.

Like I mentioned, how you choose to spend your dollars makes a big difference; and I don't mean *how much you spend*, I mean specifically "how" you spend it. For example, when you spend 12 dollars on a meal, it actually *matters* whether you spent that same money on McDonald's, or on a local family-owned restaurant. I'm not saying that every chain restaurant is bad or evil and that every locally

JUMPSTART

owned restaurant is good and ethically operated, however, if everyone goes to the big chain restaurants by default, family restaurants will struggle and eventually close, thus leading to a higher rate of monopoly. Competition is what keeps capitalism healthy and fair, therefore, always try to spend your money outside of the companies that are so large that represent a threat to fair competition. The bottom line is that we, the people, control whether monopolies are formed or not, simply by choosing where we spend our dollars. Try to spend locally as much as possible, and when you do, and tip generously if you can.

Why do you think that a tray of 12 Walmart "Great Value" eggs costs just over one dollar, while the competing brands cost at least twice as much? Do you think that the chickens are farmed in humane conditions and fed nutritious ration? How about the farmers? Walmart is so powerful that they can literally afford to lose money on a certain product or field of products, driving other competing companies out of businesses, thus taking over that share of the market for themselves. Don't get me wrong, Walmart is great, but we need to be mindful of how much we feed the beast.

For this and many other reasons, as much as possible try to spend locally, or at least, outside these huge companies that are driving others out of business. If you're not absolutely broke and can afford a little more expensive, never buy the cheapest eggs, or the cheapest anything, especially food products. In case you're struggling with money and needing to save as much as possible, by all means, get the cheapest stuff—you need to take care of yourself first! However, when you're doing a little better, don't be super stingy and choose to buy what costs a little more than the cheapest of them all. This way, you're helping to keep wages higher and, hopefully, supporting more ethical and humane business practices—it's hard to know for sure if that will actually be the case, but always buying the cheapest of the cheap stuff is a sure way to not support wages and best practices.

Let me give you a real-world example: At the time of this writing, the Wild Planet Tuna costs $2.86, whereas the StarKist tuna costs

$0.92—both are Skipjack tuna in a 5oz can. Why the hell would you pay three times more for the same freaking tuna!? Well, to begin with, the cheaper tuna is owned by the global seafood giant named "Dongwon," which is TRASHING the oceans and dragging down the whole industry—so you have both problems of monopoly and nature conservation, including animal cruelty (you may eat a little bit of dolphin and turtle with your tuna, without knowing). Also, the Wild Planet tuna is mercury safe, and they stick only to sustainable fishing practices. Now, let me ask you this, which company pays better their employees and provides better conditions for them to work? Dongwon (a.k.a. "StarKist"), or Wild Planet? The answer is obvious.

So, there you have it. When you buy the cheapest tuna, you're contributing to the expansion of the monopoly of a company that operates with unethical business practices and trashing the ocean. If everybody buys from them, soon companies with better morale and sustainable practices will disappear, and at some point, even tuna may disappear altogether by being fully extinct. This same principle applies to much of the food industry; therefore, I urge you to not buy the cheapest of the cheapest food products. Five years ago, when I had to count my dollars and was broke, did I pay three bucks for a tuna can? Of course not. Now that I have my life together, do I pay three bucks for a tuna can? Yes, I do! Like I said, **when** you can afford, don't buy the cheapest stuff—this is how you keep Earth, humanity and capitalism from falling in a downward spiral. This book is designed to get you there, to where you no longer need to buy the cheapest stuff, to where you no longer have bad debt, to where you're no longer part of the problem, but instead, an asset for the economy and part of the solution. Better capitalism starts with you and I, my friend. Let's make money in the best possible way, and then *spend* it in the best possible way as well.

When you go to a less developed capitalist country, such as Brazil, you'll see less chains and more local businesses, and in my opinion, that shows the tendency of monopolies forming in a developed capitalist system; but by choosing where we spend our money, we can

JUMPSTART

have a full blown, thriving and developed capitalist system while keeping these monopolies in check. Even with monopolies out of control, capitalism is still better than a centralized command economy, because in that case, everything belongs to the government, and that is the ultimate form of monopoly. It's up to us to keep the capitalist system in its optimum spot, where wages are higher, and morale is better.

Just like it matters *how* you spend your money, it also matters how you *make* your money—not just "how much" you make. For example, if you "make" money by day-trading stocks, you're not actually *making* anything, you're just leveraging the financial system to your advantage. If you buy stocks for $23.00 and sell them hours later for $25.00, yes, you *pulled some money out of the financial system* for yourself, but you didn't actually MAKE that money; meaning that, there's not any more money in the system, or value created because of you—that is an ethical and even legal dilemma. It becomes a legal matter when market manipulations (such as the "pump and dump" scheme) occur, but that's beside the point. If you want more info on that, just watch The Wolf of Wall Street (2013) and Boiler Room (2000), and you'll get a full picture—I am AVERSE to these practices.

That is surely the quickest way to fail capitalism, and thanks to these Wall Street Morons (WSM), we've had the awful financial crisis of 2008—again, capitalism fails when morale fails. Not all wealthy people are the same; there's an ENORMOUS difference between parasites that get rich by questionable practices like that, and those of admirable character and unwavering persistence that actually build something of value to last—such as the company I work for, that's been around for 48 years. Keep in mind that, just like not all poor people are the same, not all rich people are the same either. A generic label such as "The 1%" is very harmful, as it basically puts every "one percenter" in the same box, from the scum of wall street and corrupt bureaucrats that exploit and impoverishes people, to the hardest working and most noble successful business owners that create much needed jobs—and trust me, they're very, VERY different people.

Although I just went on a spree of bashing Wall Street, I want to emphasize that I have absolutely no problem with ethically trading stocks and taking a company public. When you create a company of value, for its great products, services, technology, etc., you're doing everyone a favor by allowing them to invest in your genuine business and gain with you. For example, if genius scientists at XYZ corporation create a new revolutionary chip and forecast lots of growth, you can choose to buy shares at their company, and should they succeed in growing, you will see proportional gains of your capital—even without knowing the first thing about making chips! Isn't that wonderful? Making gains on something that you didn't have to develop the skills for? On the same token, should they fail, you would lose your money too.

For example, Apple Inc. shares were trading for $29 in January 2017, and four years later, these same shares were trading for over $120—boy, I wish I had invested in their stocks! At the same time, General Electric stocks were trading for $30, and four years later, their shares were trading for just $11—pretty darn bad. Investing in stocks is quite risky and a bit of a gamble, unless you have a very select and excellent investing portfolio—personally, it's not for me, but it may serve you well.

On the opposite end of the stick, Creating Value (Chapter 23) is unquestionably the most constructive way that you can increase your financial gains, while at the same time, adding value and improving the health of the financial system. Maybe you get to create something so amazing, that one day, you'll be the one taking your company public and selling shares of it in the stock market. As for myself, I would much rather keep my company private, as not having to answer to multiple shareholders—and their elected board of directors—allows for a much better focus on the company culture, as well as the happiness and wellbeing of everyone in it—but that's just me!

JUMPSTART

On the flip side, there's no shortage of people that call themselves "entrepreneurs" that start a "biz" already thinking of an exit strategy. Thankfully, many of these businesses truly have value, but some of them just *appear* to have value—because the founder truly doesn't give a f*ck about it, all that he (or she) can think of, is selling the damn business for the highest possible value. When that is the case, what kind of leader (Chapter 14) do you think that the CEO is? Imagine being an employee in a company that the founder started with the intent to sell as soon as possible and for the highest possible amount of money, do you think that's a happy place to work? That's SAD. If you start a company out of your desire to create something meaningful, to be helpful, and at a later time you decide to sell it, by all means, do it! But please don't start a business exclusively thinking of selling it—that sucks.

I cannot urge you enough to create value, create value, and create value. It may be by inventing something useful, doing research, developing a technology, fixing up a house and reselling it, providing services based on your valuable skills, building a company, etc. Whenever you create value, you're playing a **positive sum game**—that is what grows the economy and effectively helps everyone. In other words, when you make your money this way, others make money too. The United States is an incredibly rich country because of the massive amounts of value created by its very creative population of both natives and immigrants. The United States has the highest influx of smart and / or hardworking people from all over the world that come here exclusively to create value—fantastic!

Whenever you manage to "make" money in any form other than creating value or rendering a service—for example, by day trading stocks, pulling off some shady scheme, or downright stealing—you're playing a **zero-sum game.** In this case, you're "making" your money at someone else's expense. I'm using quote marks, because by no means you're actually *making* any money, in this case, you just figured out a way to transfer the wealth of others into your pocket; you're enriching by making others poorer. That's what thieves do, from the highest ranked politicians and bureaucrats to the lowest pocket picking bastards on the street. Yes, I've just put a corrupt PRESIDENT, Wall Street Morons, and a Pickpocket all in the same box—they have the same flawed characters and are playing the same zero-sum game.

Particularly those that became wealthy by stealing, are the ones driving wealth inequality through the roof—In fact, I am much more disgusted by rich thieves than poor thieves; stealing is always wrong, but a rich thief has NO excuse. And to be completely honest, how could I condemn someone for stealing a piece of bread? I can't. When the belly hurts with hunger, we can do things we're not proud of. Survival supersedes values and morale, and when you're in extreme poverty, you will have no choice but to survive.

By the way, keep in mind that <u>governments can only SPEND</u> your hard-earned tax money, hopefully in exchange for a good leadership and much needed public services such as the police, court system, etc. Are you sure you want to vote for those that want to grow the government even more? Bigger government means that a bigger chunk of your money will be **withheld** to pay for *their* expenses—including private jets, mansions, iats, "massage therapists," etc... If the government cannot create any money, they cannot GIVE you "free" anything—simple! Here's a good *rule of the thumb*: legitimate business owners get rich by enriching others, while bureaucrats get rich by impoverishing others. The bigger the government, the less businessmen and more bureaucrats you'll have—and vice-versa.

Ok, on to the next point. I also believe that there is a *bell curve* to optimizing business and services, including government operations. For example, using typewriters is just counter-productive; pretty much everyone does better by using computers instead—that was a great optimization. However, when you start replacing people with Ai (artificial intelligence) in the form of robots and computers that can operate themselves, we have a problem. Before optimizing for business, **we want to optimize for people**! What good is it to optimize businesses by lowering their cost of operation, if we optimize

JUMPSTART

the people out of it? Businesses are a beautiful thing created <u>by the people, for the people</u>. I just want to make the point that I'm very weary when robots and Ai start replacing people—optimization is great only up to a certain point, but not past that.

This is a bit more of a philosophical debate, but I also STRONGLY believe in the "Earth Value" of things. For example, the price of a brand-new Honda Civic is over 40 times more than of a used 1999, and yet, both of them have about the same amount of metal, plastic, glass, etc. Older flat screen TVs use almost exactly the same exact materials as new "smart" TVs. From the *earth's point of view*, they're not that different. There's only so much we can source from earth and then dump back on it without suffering the consequences in the short time frame of less than one hundred years—yes, I've said "short." Earth will eventually recycle everything, but it takes hundreds, if not thousands of years. I'm not an environmentalist, but there's no question that we're polluting and littering way more than we should. We haven't yet truly felt the consequences of sourcing and dumping earth's resources quickly and mindlessly, but it's obvious that if we continue to do so, it will become critical. <u>If we only so much use our things for a little longer</u> before dumping it and switching over to the newest and shiniest version of it, it would lessen the littering and polluting that we're doing. By the way, please separate and recycle your trash :-)

Beyond that, if you think in terms of optimization, a production line is super optimized, whereas repair shops are not as much—remember, optimization is great, as long as we don't optimize ourselves out of it. For example, if one person in a TV factory can produce 50 televisions, one person in a repair shop may be able to fix just two or three TVs a day; therefore, if we keep our things a little longer, there will be more repair shops in business and more people employed. Yet in this example, the production line worker building the 50 televisions is just doing repetitive work, whereas the technician at the repair shop is actually figuring things out and using his brain, because every broken TV is different—that's an important distinction.

By exercising his (or her) intellect, the technician is probably happier, and has a higher chance of one day inventing something of value. Personally, I'm proud to be driving used cars and to have bought much of my stuff second hand—it all works great! We should always purchase new technology that serves us better, but I think it would be a good thing to use our stuff a little longer before dumping it in a landfill. That's just MY opinion, ok?

Yet with the pollution and littering in mind, I also strongly believe that we need to make way for a SHARING economy. Imagine this, in a condo with 12 houses, does everyone run their lawnmowers every single day!? OBVIOUSLY not. So, why the heck does every single homeowner in that condo, at a walking distance from each other, have a lawnmower? They could simply buy two lawnmowers, then each one of them could use the lawnmower every other week for two days, and yet, there would be enough idle time to service it; but instead, everyone is paying in full for their own lawnmower, as well as the maintenance of it. Moving into the future where littering and pollution is a growing issue, I think we will have no choice but to make way for a sharing economy, in order to reduce the footprint of our pollution and littering. Personally, I hate to see my lawnmower sitting in the garage for over 300 days of the year, when someone could be using it as well—it makes no sense! Let me know if you want to borrow my lawnmower, I'll be happy to let you use the damn thing.

Lastly, the best you can do right now, is to simply manage your money well (Chapter 21). When you have savings and don't have specifically the *bad kind of debt*, you're an asset to the economy. The second-best thing you can do right now, is to help someone else get their finances in order, by educating them about the different kinds of debt, how to budget, etc. Why the hell doesn't school teach us that!? Anyway... When we, individually, are doing well and using our money responsibly, the economy is good and stable. By taking care of your finances, you're taking care of everyone that participates in the economy.

JUMPSTART

Recommended Watch on YouTube:

The Call of an Entrepreneur
How creating value benefits everyone in the financial system.
In the Age of AI
The dark side of optimization and the dangers of government control using A.I.

Motivational Quotes

and

Nuggets of Wisdom

Quotes and Wisdom

By the Author

1 - Genuine success is not only based on one's accomplishments, but also greatly based on one's overcomings.

2 - If it's a problem that can be solved, then it's not a problem, but just a small inconvenience.

3 - We can't immediately have what we want, but we can always make the best of what we have.

4 - Offering help is only good to the extent that you don't make the receiving person feel awkward to refuse it.

5 - When you do your best work, you're not only serving others, but you're serving yourself.

6 - Do not tell the world what you can do. Show it instead.

7 - Employees respond to the mass mentality of a company just like the cells of our bodies respond to our state-of-mind. Thus for a happy and productive workplace, it is of utmost importance to have energizing, positive leaders.

7 – The difference between a workaholic and someone who loves to work starts with their set of values and ends with their legacy; whereas one wants to escape the world, the other wants to contribute and create something good that transcends his (or her) existence.

Quotes and Wisdom

By other Authors and Leaders

1 - "The only man who makes no mistakes is the man who never does anything. Do not be afraid of mistakes provided you do not make the same mistake twice." — Roosevelt

2 - "You will never know your capacity for achievement, until you mix your efforts with imagination." — Napoleon Hill

3 - "Enthusiasm is great, but persistence is what will get you there." — Steve Irby

4 - "Profit from failure. It is a tool for learning, not an outcome." — Scott Adams

5 - "Struggle is a main advantage, it develops talents and abilities which would remain dormant otherwise." — Napoleon Hill

5 - "Creative thought is a killer for misery, not the cause of it. The cause of misery is a situation in which the individual lives below the level of his own humanity." — Manly P. Hall

6 - "The policies that support self-esteem are the policies that make money." — Nathaniel Branden

8 - "Throw away the hammer and quit knocking, the big prizes of life go to the builders and not the destroyers." — Napoleon Hill

9 - "Every addiction starts with pain and ends with pain." — Unknown Author

10 - "Self-discipline is self-love." — Will Smith

11 - "If you believe you must watch every word so you never say the wrong thing, you may never say the right thing." — John Bradshaw

JUMPSTART

12 - "The way we handle our problems determines the quality of our lives." — John Bradshaw

13 - "One way to forgive and forget our enemies is to become absorbed in some cause infinitely bigger than ourselves." — Dale Carnegie

14 - "I measure my accomplishments not by how tired I am at the end of the day, but how tired I am not." — Daniel W. Josselyn

15 - "Failing doing what you don't love hurts more than failing doing what you love." — Jim Carrey.

16 - "The bottom line in leadership isn't how far we advance ourselves, but how far we advance others." — John C Maxwell.

17 - "You are only as strong and extraordinary as you give yourself reason to be." — Brendon Burchard

18 - "Pessimistic people get to be right, optimistic people get to be rich." — Unknown author.